BERTHA VENATION

BERTHA VENATION

And Hundreds of Other
Funny Names of Real People

LARRY ASHMEAD

P

PROFILE BOOKS

First published in Great Britain in 2007 by
Profile Books Ltd
3a Exmouth House
Pine Street
Exmouth Market
London EC1R 0JH
www.profilebooks.com

First published in the United States of America in 2007 by HarperCollins Publishers

1 3 5 7 9 10 8 6 4 2

Designed by Laura Lindgren

"The God of Large Cheques" reproduced by kind permission of *Private Eye*.
"Queen Victoria and 'those four-footed friends no bride can buy'" copyright © 2000
by Paul Johnson.

Printed and bound in Great Britain by Clays, Bungay, Suffolk

A CIP catalogue record for this book is available from the British Library.

ISBN 978 1 86197 717 5

The paper this book is printed on is certified by the © 1996 Forest Stewardship
Council A.C. (FSC). It is ancient-forest friendly. The printer holds FSC chain of custody
SGS-COC-2061

FSC
Mixed Sources
Product group from well-managed
forests and other controlled sources

Cert no. SGS-COC-2061
www.fsc.org
© 1996 Forest Stewardship Council

This book is dedicated to
Walter Mathews,
best friend for forty-two years

CONTENTS

INTRODUCTION

I have always been fascinated by names. I don't know why.
I grew up as Lawrence Peel Ashmead, the second child in
an ordinary family in Rochester, New York. My father was
named Lawrence Henry, my mother Lillian (Peel was her
maiden name). My older brother is Thomas Graham. But
all around me were other names, different, funny, even
remarkable names.

My mother's two best friends were Edith Shortsleeve and
Bettina Buttons.

During a high school football game so important the
coach was on the field rather than at his wife's side in the
delivery room, twins were born just after halftime and over
the loudspeaker the father proclaimed: "Ladies and gentle-
men, I've got a Razzle and a Dazzle!"

A neighbor made a fortune in bottled tomato sauce and put
a sign in front of his new home: "The House that Ragu Built."
Just down the street another sign proclaimed, "Deja View."
My high school mathematics teacher retired to a cottage in
the country, named Aftermath. I've always loved imaginative names of houses. Years later, in the 1970s, I was not to be
denied. I bought a beach house on the ocean in the Hamptons
and named it Lay-Me-Dune. The house later washed away in
a hurricane but the name is immortalized in novels by Susan
Isaacs, Anne Rivers Siddons, and Celestine Sibley.

When I began working at Simon and Schuster the Human Resources Department mistakenly thought my name was Lawrence P. Ashead. Despite many complaints I couldn't get anyone to correct the error. For the year and a half I remained at the publishing house this was my official name on security passes, paychecks, medical forms—any piece of paper originating from the Human Resources Department. During college I worked at the Eastman Kodak company. Here my name was spelled correctly.

Simon and Schuster, perhaps a giant in the publishing world but tiny in the business world, made a mistake and couldn't or wouldn't correct it. I thought it was mean-spirited; my mother was outraged by the cavalier attitude toward what she considered a highly regarded surname. My father laid all blame at the feet of the newfangled computer. Sam Vaughan, a wise mentor at Doubleday, got it right. With a sense of foreboding he thought it was a harbinger of the coming conglomeration of small companies and a reflection of the diminishing importance of the editor in the world of book publishing.

My mother was a great fan of the television show *Dynasty* and she particularly admired Alexis Carrington, played by Joan Collins, a smart knowledgeable business-woman. It was over-the-top in melodrama, especially in its repartee on the telephone. My mother was not in business but she was an astoundingly quick-take. She lived in Upstate New York and rarely called me at my office. Once, when *Dynasty* was the most popular drama on television, she had some good reason to call.

My assistant was Court VanRooten.

Court: "Mr. Ashmead's office."

Mother: "Is he there?"

Court: "I'm sorry, he is in a meeting. May I take your name?"

Mother: "Please tell him his mother called. He'll know who it is."

My mother was very proud of our surname. If her marriage had taken place in a more modern era I'm sure she would have linked a hyphen to her family name Peel, but

Ashmead was unique enough to shore up her fragile sense of elitism. She also took pride in her discovery of an heirloom apple, Ashmead's Kernel, developed in England in the 1770s. She ignored the fact that it was described as "ugly by modern standards." She wasn't aggressive, just a bit of a snob upstate where common names were, well, common.

When I moved to New York in 1960 my driver's license was about to expire. I hightailed it to the motor vehicle bureau on Worth Street. The clerk editing my renewal form casually commented, "Ashmead, that's my married name." "Really, it is such an uncommon name." "Not in Harlem, lots of Ashmeads up there." A few days later I recalled this conversation to my mother. She obviously thought this put a bit of a puncture in her overinflated idea of the exclusivity of the Ashmead name but recovered quickly. "I presume your father's ancestors had many slaves. Upon their release to freedom they had no last names, and welcomed the surname Ashmead."

At one point in the early 1960s my mother called me to say she'd seen Bennett Cerf on television, also Jacqueline Susann. Did I know them? Did I know any famous authors? I proudly told her I counted Isaac Asimov as one of my own. She said, "That's an odd name, Isaac Asimov. He sounds Jewish." I said, "Yes, he is." "Well, remember, he's smarter than you are."

One more Mother story—it doesn't involve a funny name but a wonderful malapropism. Edith Delinsky was my mother's best friend for many years. Edith was a worldwide traveler. Rochester offered Edith little adventure. Canada, only a few miles to the north, was fine for skiing but that was a sport for the younger set. She and a few lady friends, all with up-to-date passports and airline-approved suitcases with wheels, would leave their husbands and travel the globe. Husbands stayed at their jobs at Kodak. Wives took the family camera and brought back countless Kodachrome slides for endless evenings of neighborly entertainment. Edith, the most intrepid of the group, was especially fond of taking photographs of dishes of food as it was served and after eating.

Years later I said to my mother, "You haven't mentioned Edith in a long time. Does she still take those long trips?" My mother lowered her voice, customary when talking about serious subjects, especially illness. "Poor Edith. Her kidneys are almost completely shot. I can't help but think it was all those foreign foods she ate. But those days are gone. Edith is practically intercontinental."

On my first trip to London I stayed at the Londoner Hotel in Welbeck Street. Registered at the same time was a Lady Ashmead and, after a bit of confusion at the switchboard, I rang her. "There are so few Ashmeads," I said to her. "Perhaps we should meet. We could be related." "I doubt it very much," was her curt reply.

On this same visit to London I made the rounds of the book publishers. There were many companies before the great and small mergers that took place in the 1980s. One of the most distinguished was Collins. The company was

scattered in a series of connected town houses on St. James'
Place. It was owned by the Collinses, a family with an
illustrious Scottish background. I had a midmorning meeting with Lady Collins, affectionately known to her friends
as Pierre. I dressed spiffily to impress her, hoping she'd be
more agreeable than Lady Ashmead had been. Indeed, she
was most pleasant and she offered me a cup of tea and a
plate of Walker's ginger cookies. After a few words about
the weather she looked at me with a hard eye and asked,
"That Royal Stewart tie is lovely. Are you entitled to wear
it?" "I don't think so. I bought it because I like the colors."
"As an old-fashioned Scot I really don't approve of the
untitled wearing of a tartan. At the risk of offense I ask you
to remove it. I'll reimburse you of course and you can go to
a very nice clothing shop just around the corner in Jermym
Street." As I left she gave me a couple of pounds and I promised never to wear a tartan again. I haven't.

When I was nine years old I attended a talk at the school
library. Her name was Amber Dean, a mystery writer who
lived in Avon, New York. I don't remember the title of the
book but I do remember that she said she typed her manuscript and sent it off to her editor at Doubleday, who read
it in her office in a skyscraper in New York City, and that
nine months later there was a finished book. The words
were imprinted in my mind. I loved to read and reading in a
skyscraper in New York sounded a lot more interesting than
reading in Rochester. Of course at nine years old I couldn't
follow up, but twenty-one years later I did. I turned down

a job as a geologist in Texas and went to New York City to become a book editor. It was the only major, life-changing decision I ever made and it was the right one. It was sheer coincidence that I was hired by Doubleday, and that editor I'd heard about twenty-one years previously was still reading in her office in a skyscraper. Her name was Isabelle Taylor and we soon became colleagues and close friends. A few years later Isabelle retired after more than forty years. On the day of her retirement party Nelson Doubleday, the son of the founder of the company, which was still family owned, called me into his office and asked me to go to Tiffany's and pick out a nice present for Isabelle. (He called beforehand and authorized my purchase.) I knew I was earning more than Isabelle (women in book publishing made far less than men at the time) and I realized this was my opportunity to at least try to level the playing field. I bought her a beautiful amethyst bracelet for $21,000. At the party that evening she said how much she loved Doubleday and young Nelson, adding that she would have paid them to have worked there. It was the perfect gift and Nelson never questioned the cost.

As my interest in names grew I realized how important they are. Names are distinctive marks of individuality that set everyone off from almost everyone else. My passion is for names that are unusual, extraordinary, and often humorous. I have collected funny names most of my life and I loved *Remarkable Names of Real People or How to Name Your Baby*, by John Train, when it was published in 1979. So did Andrew Franklin, a British publisher. He knew about my fondness for most things offbeat and quirky, especially names, and suggested I take an entirely new, up-to-date look at the subject. I hope you'll enjoy this compilation of names as much as I've enjoyed collecting them.

BERTHA VENATION

CHAPTER 1

ᑲᕆ

BRITNEY WHO?:
WHATEVER HAPPENED TO
MARY AND JOHN?

From the maximonline.com Web site come quotes from Kid Rock and George Carlin that may influence the way some parents decide to name their baby boys.

Kid Rock: "Chicks come up to me and say, 'Oh Kid Rock, what's your real name?' It's Bob. They're like, 'That's it? Couldn't you have a cool name?' Nope. My parents still call me Bob. If my mom starts calling me Rock, I'll fucking flip" (from March 2002).

George Carlin: "I hate guys named Todd. I think that's a goofy fucking name. All the boy names that have come along—Taylor, Tucker, Carlson, Cassidy, Cody, Flynn— they're not real names. A real name is Jim" (from June 2001).

◎

I thought the use of the same old names (John, Edward, Mary, Susan) showed a distinct conformity and lack of imagination among recent generations. But that has changed and it seems we have gone too far the other way. For example, here's a recent list of babies born in Upstate New York.

Caiden Lee
Tyler Ryan
Carly Morgan
Jeremiah James Jr.
Sarafia Frances
Brianna Darcie
Hayles Tasha
Sabryn Maura
Bethanyann Busta
Kai Nolan
Autumn Elizabeth
Ashlywn Zoe
Trinity Jade

Bette Harrison, who keeps an eye on new arrivals at O'Grady Hospital in Atlanta, spotted Vaseline Glass.

A baby boy was born in the backseat of his parents' car. They named him Car Radio, later shortened to Cardio.

:|

A piece in *The* (London) *Times* (October 26, 2004) by Gary Slapper reported that a father from Zhengzhou, Henan Province, in China wanted to name his child "@." According to Slapper, the father was denied "on the legal basis that all names must be capable of being translated into Mandarin." He also reports that English law is not as strict, and that "After Michael Howerd, of Leeds, had been charged £20 by his bank for a £10 overdraft excess, he changed his name by deed poll to Yorkshire Bank plc Are Fascist Bastards."

:P

OOPS! DEPARTMENT
From the Ithaca (N.Y.) Journal.

Prentice Smith and Kenna Lindsey, Newfield, a daughter, Fatima Rene, March 26, 2003. (Rene has an accent mark, but I don't know how to process one with this program. David Durrett)

THE NEW YORKER, JANUARY 17, 2005

The ethnic population of New York City has been changing rapidly in the past decade. Jennifer 8. Lee reported in
the *New York Times*: "In the last several years, New York
City has had more baby girls named Fatoumata than Lisa,
more Aaliyahs than Melissas, more Chayas than Christinas.
There have been more baby boys named Moshe than Peter,
more Miguels than Jeffreys, more Ahmeds than Stanleys....
But the reverse also happens. Jose and Luis were the top two
names for Hispanic baby boys in 1980. But today they have
slipped out of the Top 10, behind names like Brandon, Kevin
and Christopher."

Note: Jennifer 8. Lee's unusual name is explained in
chapter 4.

In the May 13, 2007, Sunday *New York Times*, Tony
Allen-Mills reported that parents are increasingly going to
Google when deciding what to name their children. One
mother named her son Finn*egan J*ames (asterisks inten-
tional) "so her blog entries would not start showing up in
Internet searches for James Joyce or *Finnegan's Wake*.

From Bryan Oettel

A mother wanted to call her son Sheatodd, but spelled it
"Shithead." It took a social worker to come in and convince
her not to name her son that way.

!

From Denise L. McIver

    Tupac Amaru Shakur, deceased rapper

    Jedi Mahedi Moore, her partner's grandson (named after characters in *Star Wars*)

⚡

Radar (September/October 2005) reported some popular, unusual baby names for 2006 (found at alternativebaby-names.com). Among them:

Cadley

Faxon

Jaeger

Lathe

Lazer

Quade

Race

Tage

Wakely

Zealand

Sarah Crichton at Farrar, Straus and Giroux, who is editing a book that Starbucks has chosen to sell in its stores, made this contribution.

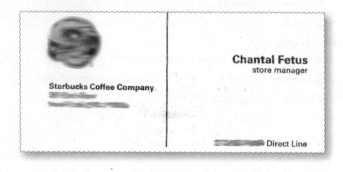

Craig Westling supplied the names of childhood friends given by their hippie parents:

Miklos Thunderbolt

Corrina Wildflower

Kaya Sequoia

Canyon

Genghis

Nimpkish

Bear

Trodat (last name Fishback)

Ellen McClelland-Lesser told me these:

Skier Picabo Street's younger brother is named Juan Way Street.

Her friend Lynne Odell spent two summers at a ranch in Colorado, where she met Bird Durrance and her younger sister Worm.

A ballet dancer is named Benjamin Millipied.

A surgeon named Dr. Thomas Gouge operates at New York University Medical Center.

Cyril Sapiro, a Toronto trustee in bankruptcy, sent me an essay on his experiences as a specialist lawyer and I quote: "Some of our bankrupts are burdened with unusual names. Surnames like Clodd, Noseworthy, Pickles and Smellie are matters of public record. But giving a child a first name like Egbert, Bernight, Blondine, Hazal, Philbert or Pursglove is cruel—an open invitation to a bloody nose in a school playground."

From Jeff Shapiro

A little girl in Sante Fe, child of hippies, was named Sunset and wanted to be called Cathy.

From Amy Scheibe, via Leslie Meredith

"My sister told me of a little girl in her class named Heaven. This happened in gym class last week: the girls were helping each other do sit-ups in pairs and the teacher said to one little girl, 'Scoot your body closer to Heaven.' They all laughed."

Will Schwalbe's friend in Hong Kong is called Sugar Tong. (*Tong* means "sugar," so his name is really Sugar Sugar, or Tong Tong, depending on how you translate it.)

( )

From Will Swift

On Long Island, the nine Fluck children were referred to as Flock of Flucks. Also, twins named for islands: Catalina (girl), known as Cat, and Kitt (boy), known as Kit.

!

A hospital in Upstate New York included the following in their birth announcements:

Le'ondre Jessie James
Mone't Elysea Ann
Da' Mazion Ced' Yanii
Anief Dre-cere
Diamond Lanae Nemiah
Nayraha Dmarye
Giacomo Hooch
Jayden Xavier

More babies born in Upstate New York in February of 2005:

Desire Paris
Ky'shon Mazeak
Cha-Narion Maquise
Kody Ryan
Tajae Nylei
Kobe A
Nyeerah Oqay-lyn

Roland Philipps, managing director of John Murray, publishers in the UK, contributed these:

"My wife, Felicity Rubinstein, was at school with two girls: Raine Shine (first name pronounced as if it had an 'r' on the end) and Lavender Hanky.

My sister had a car she named Flattery, because it got her nowhere."

☺

Josef Asteinza, a designer and architect, remembers these names:

Cinnamon Booth, now believed to be a TV producer.

Retired archbishop of Manila Jaime Sin used the Catholic convention of placing a title between first and last names, and so was known as Jaime Cardinal Sin.

Tressy Miller, whose real name was Enchantress.

Branch Woodburn, a stage actor in New York City.

Increase Mather and his son Cotton, Massachusetts Bay colonists.

Josef also remembers a college philosophy professor named Alfonso Lingus. His wife, named Connie, was a Latin teacher who addressed students by their surnames: Master Change, Master Jones. That stopped when she got to a student named Paul Bader.

🚫

Mary Tobin Adams Hedges was a dear friend in the late 1960s and '70s when I owned a beach house in Sagaponack, a small town in the Hamptons. My three cats loved the freedom of the dunes planted with back pine, dune grass, and beach plum bushes. I decided to find a cat sitter for the days when I wasn't there. I ran an ad in the local paper. Mary Hedges called and stopped by with her two golden retrievers. The dogs and cats became instant friends. Mary Hedges was an astoundingly elegant woman with the kind of comfortable bearing you couldn't buy at Bailey & Huebner in Southampton, New York, or any smart shop in Paris. My partner, Walter Mathews, and I fell under her spell and she became an important part of our lives for more than a decade until she died in the early eighties.

How does this story of a good friend fit into this book on funny names? I recently read a current best seller, *Freakonomics* by Levitt and Dubner. The authors mention the case of Temptress, a teenaged girl who was under scrutiny of Albany County family court for ungovernable behavior, which included bringing men home while the mother was at work. She was given the name by her mother, who liked a young actress on *The Cosby Show* named Tempestt Bledsoe but misspelled the name.

The authors pose this question: "Does the name you give your child affect his life? Or is it *your* life reflected in his name? In either case, what kind of signal does a child's name send to the world—and most important, does it really matter?"

To return briefly to Mary Hedges. Her first marriage was to Casswell Adams, a noted sportswriter for the *New York Herald Tribune*. On the occasion of a sports award dinner at the Waldorf-Astoria, Mary was seated opposite the handsome and very charming Joe DiMaggio. During the course of the awards ceremony Mary saw Mr. DiMaggio take out a small notebook. He scribbled something on a page, tore it out, and quietly passed it to her. Later in the ladies' room she unfolded the note and read the one-word message:

TEMPTRESS!

The note was one of Mary's proudest possessions. Much later she showed it to me and I thought it was the perfect emblem of an earlier, romantic time when celebrities, even sports celebrities, were not only handsome and charming but graceful and discreet.

CHAPTER 2

❧

APPLE TO ZOWIE:
CELEBRITIES ARE
MAJOR OFFENDERS

Moon Unit Zappa has three siblings, Dweezil, Ahmet, and Diva. Here's a list of other children of celebrities given odd names.

Zowie Bowie (David and Angie Bowie)

Rolan Bolan (Mark Bolan and Gloria Jones)

Peaches Honeyblossom and Pixie (Bob Geldoff and Paula Yates), also half sister Heavenly Hiraany Tiger Lily (Michael Hutchence and Paula Yates)

China god Slick (Paul Kantner and Grace Slick)

Dandelion Pallenberg (Keith Richards and Anita Pallenberg)

Elija Bob Patricius Guggi Q Hewson (Bono and Ali Hewson)

Moxie CrimeFighter and Zolten Penn (Penn Jillette and wife Emily Zolten)

Pilot Inspector Riesgraf Lee (Jason Lee and Beth Riesgraf)

Banjo (Rachel Griffiths and Andrew Taylor)

Audio Science (son of Shannyn Sossamon of *A Knight's Tale*)
Coco Arquette (Courtney Cox and David Arquette)
Maddox, Zahara, Shiloh, and Pax Pitt-Jolie (Angelina Jolie and Brad Pitt)

Gwyneth Paltrow and Chris Martin followed the celebrity tradition for unusual names and came up with Apple for their first daughter. Recently, on *Oprah*, Ms. Paltrow said the name fuss caught her by surprise. When she hears "Apple," she thinks "sweet and wholesome."

Here's what happened to another Apple born thirty-three years ago, reported in a letter to the *New York Times*:

> I too was a counterculture parent, and 33 years ago I named my daughter Apple. When she was in elementary school, she got teased a lot, and like Strawberry Saroyan, she tried to change her name in junior high. However, by then, she could not relate to being called anything but Apple, so she kept her name and eventually grew to enjoy the attention.
>
> My daughter didn't grow up in a liberal, progressive community, but those of us living the hippie life all gave our kids unusual names, so she was in good company.

(One of my best friends named her girls Snowflake and Raspberry.) A year or two after my daughter was born, my then-husband discovered that Johnny Appleseed (John Chapman) was in his family tree. So when people ask my daughter how she got such an unusual name, she can tell them about Johnny Appleseed instead of saying her parents were just crazy hippies.

BARBARA CHAPMAN
Rapid City, South Dakota

Some readers may remember the popular young actress of thirty years ago named Barbara Hershey Seagull. A hippie name if there ever was one. If you look up Barbara today, the name on her doorbell reads simply "Hershey." The seagull has flown.

And the list goes on.

Makena'lei Gordon (Helen Hunt)

Elijah Blue (Cher and Gregg Allman)

Poppy Honey and Daisy Boo (daughters of celebrity chef Jamie Oliver and wife Jools)

Rumer (after novelist Rumer Godden), Scout (after the narrator of *To Kill a Mockingbird*), and Tallulah Belle Willis (daughters of Bruce Willis and Demi Moore)

Director Kevin Smith has a daughter named Harley
Quinn, after the *Batman* character

Bluebell Madonna Halliwell (daughter of former Spice
Girl Geri Halliwell)

Chilli Jade Evans (child of Hugo chef Peter Evans and
Astrid Edlinger)

Jack Ryan's Title Tattle™ *Post Chronicle* online article, "No
Red Rose: Tom Cruise's Suri More Likely Fiery Boy's Name,"
shows that Tom Cruise and Katie Holmes may have missed
the mark in naming their little girl Suri. Citing a piece in the
New York *Daily News*, he tells us that according to Professor
Hooshang Amirahmadi, director for Middle Eastern stud-
ies at Rutgers University, Suri doesn't mean "red rose" in
Persian or Farsi. Amirahmadi says, "In Farsi, it [Suri] means
red, like a fiery color, but there is no such a thing as a 'suri'
that means 'red rose.'" Interestingly enough, according to
Amirahmadi, Suri can also mean "a party or celebration."
So is it Hebrew? Ryan tells us that "Hebrew language expert
Avshalom Kor told Army Radio there is only a slight con-
nection between the name Suri and the Hebrew language.
Kor said it can be a nickname for Sarah as pronounced by
Jews from Central Europe, but that Sarah in Hebrew is the
feminine form of the word for lord. In modern Hebrew, the
word means a Cabinet Minister."

One is left to wonder what Suri means in Scientology.

About the name Brad Pitt and Angelina Jolie chose for their daughter Shiloh Nouvel, Cleveland reporter Chuck Yarborough wonders: "What is up with that name? Yeah, yeah, I know the accepted story is that it means peace, and that it's mentioned in the Bible as a place in ancient Palestine where the Israelites found sanctuary. But to me, it's a Civil War battle. If this trend keeps up, little Shiloh may someday find herself in a play date with her pal Gettysburg, and the twins Bull Run I and Bull Run II over at the Appomattox Court House Little Friends Center."

Wackiest Celebrities' Kids' Names from VH1:

Phineas and Hazel (twins born to Julia Roberts and Danny Moder)

Denim and Diesel (sons of Toni Braxton and husband Carey Lewis)

Saffron Sahara, Amber Rose, Tulula Pine (daughters of Simon Le Bon and wife Yasmin)

True Isabella Summer, Sonnet, and Ocean (children of Forest Whitaker and wife)

Magnus and Mattias Ferrell (sons of Will Ferrell and wife Vivica)

Rebel, Robe, Racer, and Rocket (sons of director Robert Rodriguez and Elizabeth Avalon)

Reign Beau and Freedom (daughter and son of Ving
Rhames)

God'iss Love Stone and Heaven (daughters of hip hop
singer Lil' Moe)

Puma and Seven (daughters of Erykah Badu)

Hopper Jack Penn (son of Sean and Robin Wright Penn,
named for Dennis Hopper and Jack Nicholson)

Michael Jackson's children Prince Michael Jr., Paris
Michael, Prince Michael II—aka Blanket

Jermajesty Jackson (son of Jermaine Jackson)

Dixie Dot, Baby Belle (daughters of hip hop stars Genu-
wine and Soleil)

London and Cash (sons of Guns N' Roses guitarist Slash)

William Lear Jr. (of Learjet) named his daughter Shanda
Lear

The first real celebrity I remember was Moondog, a well-
known street person who was a fixture on the streets of
Manhattan. His customary post was at Fifty-fourth Street
and Sixth Avenue, where he stood dressed as a Viking with
a horned helmet and a spear. Moondog was born in 1916
in Kansas. He lost his sight in a dynamite explosion but
managed to pick up admirable musical knowledge. When
he arrived in New York City in 1942 he was considered a
good luck charm among certain musicians. For thirty years,

despite the weather, he would stand on his corner begging
and offering bits of his poetry or giving readings. Most of us
regarded him as a true New York eccentric.

I lived on the East Side of Manhattan during Moondog's
reign and would often swing by to check him out. He was
always there and it gave me pleasure to exchange a few
words with him. I was genuinely surprised to read his 1999
obituary in the *New York Times*. He hadn't been a landmark
on his midtown corner since the seventies but he'd been
busy. He teamed up with the likes of Julie Andrews and
Charlie Mingus and was befriended by Igor Stravinsky.
He left for Europe in 1974 and lived with a woman named
Ghirtz five years his junior who managed his career and
his more conventional garb. He performed his elaborate
compositions all over the continent. (This information
about Moondog comes from an article by Daniel Alarcón
published in the summer 2005 issue of *The Oxford
American*.)

In her October 3, 2005, widely syndicated column, Liz
Smith shared this quote from Beyoncé's mom, Tina. "I saw
Chris Rock on TV and he said, 'Black people make 10 steps
forward, and then we take 12 steps back… After "Roots" we
had Kunta, and then what do we do? We go and name our
kids "Beyoncé."' I just laughed because I'm sure he thought

it was a name I made up like Tanifa or something. He didn't
know it was my (maiden) name."

The November 24, 2006, edition of the New York *Daily
News* reported the birth of a son for supermodel Heidi Klum
and Seal: Johan Riley Fyodor Taiwo Samuel. "It is the second
child for the couple in 14 months. Their son Henry Guen-
ther Ademola Dashtu Samuel was born Sept. 12, 2005."

Whew! And Lawrence was an odd name when I was
born. I couldn't be called Larry as nicknames were not
allowed in my family, but our housekeeper Hilda called me
"Toasty" because of my fondness for toast. One friend, the
vivacious Gloria Adelson, also calls me Toasty as a tribute to
my heritage (and continuing love of toast).

This famous letter was sent to me by Antony Harwood.

H.M. EMBASSY
MOSCOW

Lord Pembroke
The Foreign Office
LONDON

6 April
1943

My Dear Reggie,

        In these dark days man tends to look for little shafts
of light that spill from heaven. My days are probably darker
than yours, and I need, my God I do, all the light I can get.
But I am a decent fellow, and I do not want to be mean and
selfish about what little brightness is shed upon me from time
to time. So I propose to share with you a tiny flash that has
illuminated my somber life and tell you that God has given
me a new Turkish colleague whose card tells me that he is
called Mustapha Kunt.

We all feel like that, Reggie, now and then, especially when
spring is upon us, but few of us would care to put it on our
cards. It takes a Turk to do that.

Sir Archibald Clerk Kerr,
H. M. Ambassador

Da Romano Trattoria in Burano, Italy, lists the many celebrities who have dined there including:

Farah Fawcet Mayor
Olive Brien
Katherine Hapburne

CHAPTER 3

THAT'S A MOUTHFUL: NAMES THAT ARE DIFFICULT TO PRONOUNCE

Isaac Asimov was one of my favorite authors I've ever worked with. I joined Doubleday as an editorial assistant in 1960 and Isaac and I discovered our mutual love of science and science fiction. In fifteen years we worked together on forty-four books. Isaac had already published *The Intelligent Man's Guide to Science* for Arthur Rosenthal at Basic Books. When we wanted to use that title for his two-volume guide to the Bible, Arthur put up a red flag. I proposed to Isaac that we call it *Asimov's Guide to the Bible*. He told me that when he first started publishing in the early 1950s, a number of people advised him to use a pseudonym, that his name was too "foreign" for the American reader. Isaac stood his ground. He was proud of his name and now here he was— not the name above the title but part of the title. We went on to publish *Asimov's Guide to Shakespeare*, *Asimov's Annotated Don Juan*, and many other fine similarly titled books.

Art Asia Pacific is a magazine covering contemporary oriental art. In its column "Whispering Gallery" we are told that Zhang Xiaogang is the name of a famed Chinese artist and that Xiaoming Zhang is another. Also, Wei Dong's work has been featured at New York's Plum Blossom Gallery.

In the June 3, 2007, Albany *Times-Union*, Tristan Stewart-Robinson has a piece titled "British museum honors American Indians who changed history," which cites the names of four leaders of the Iroquois Confederacy:

Tee Yee Neen Ho Ga Row, emperor of the Six Nation

Sa Ga Yeath Qua Pieth Tow, king of the Maquas

Ho Nee Yeath Ta No Row, king of the Generethgarich

Etow Oh Koam, king of the River Nation

It's no fun going through life correcting people on the pronunciation of your name. Columnist Harry V. Wade tells about a gentleman of importance in Egypt whose name is Asiz Esset. "His name can be pronounced by opening a soda bottle slowly."

Irene Feszczyszyn is the administratrix of the estate of Laroslaw Feszczyszyn. George Costello comments, "Obviously her grandfather was sneezing when they asked for his name at Ellis Island."

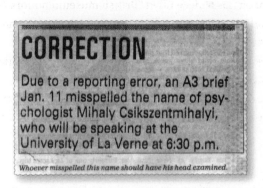

CORRECTION

Due to a reporting error, an A3 brief Jan. 11 misspelled the name of psychologist Mihaly Csikszentmihalyi, who will be speaking at the University of La Verne at 6:30 p.m.

Whoever misspelled this name should have his head examined.

From a foreclosure notice in the *New York Observer*, February 13, 2006: Suwineetha G. Gunasekera.

From Mark Lawless

Loolwa Khazzoom: founder and director of the Jewish Multicultural Project and author of *The Flying Camel and Other Essays*.

CHAPTER 4

GOING TO EXTREMES: HILARIOUSLY LONG AND MEANINGLESS BUT EFFICIENT NAMES

I'll start off with a very funny quote from a Smiley Anders column: "Judi Exner Parker of Denham Springs recalls the time two U.S. senators, William B. Sprong and Hiram Fong, sponsored a bill recommending the ringing of church bells all over the country to hail the arrival in Hong Kong of the U.S. table tennis team after its tour in China.

Unfortunately, their effort failed, depriving Congress of the opportunity to pass the Sprong-Fong Hong Kong Ping-Pong Ding-Dong bill."

MUCH TOO LONG

Seventy-something Elizabeth Harris sent me this letter about two figures of yesteryear.

Here are a couple of real people's names—culled from
my late mother's endless collection of dear friends. I am
in my 70s now, and these names are from my mother's
very frisky young ladyhood in the late 1920s and later
her marvelous high-jinks period of 1940s Hollywood.

Louis Plimpton Alabaster—scion of privilege in
the golden era of new Southern California wealth
(oranges, oil and banking). Louis was one of my
mother's numerous boyfriends, played the saxo-
phone, and his elegant portrait photograph shows
him to have an Arrow collar profile, wavy parted
hair, a soulful smile...and he signed the photo "To
my Gilly...I'll remember!" In her later years, Mother
remembered Louis as having great looks and (her
words) a tiny, tiny mind.

Peggy Berlini Lockhart Brown Lockhart Hill...
Peggy was a rivetingly pretty woman, née Berlini, who
married the actor Gene Lockhart *twice*. She claimed to
have married him the second time as a kind of sorbet
or palate cleanser after the dreary Mr. Brown (a stock-
broker) bored her half to death. Hill, her last husband,
was a calm and rather sedate businessman. Peggy
had only one child out of all the husbands, whose
name I only recall phonetically (never saw it written)
as "Jhonnkay." I was dragooned into playing with her
and remember her as being fat, ferocious and given to
hysterical screams and door-slamming.

Toot was the name adopted by an Indian originally called
Shrieking-Loud-Train-Whistle.

Famed New York literary scout Marialina Sara Allesandra
Barra di Giovanni di Santa Severina is known to one and all
as Maria Campbell.

Dr. Will Swift, author of *The Roosevelts and the Royals,* is a
walking library of the names of European royalty. Here are
a few of the longer names.

   Children of King Alfonso III of Spain and Queen Victoria Eugenie (granddaughter of Queen Victoria through
her youngest daughter Beatrice): HRH Infante Alfonso Pio
Cristino Eduardo Francisco Guillermo Enrique Eugenio
Fernando Antonio Venancio of Spain, Prince of the Asturias
(1907–38); a hemophiliac, he died in a car accident. HRH
Infante Jaime Luitpold Isabeline Enrique Alejandro Alberto
Alfonso Victor Acacio Pedro Pablo Maria of Spain, Duke
of Segovia (1908–75); he renounced the throne because of
physical infirmities. HRH Infanta Beatriz Isabel Federica
Alfonsa Eugenia Cristina Maria Teresia Bienvenida Ladislaa
of Spain (1909–2002).

   Another descendant of George III: HRH Duchess Marie-
Therese Nadejda Albertine Rosa Phillppine Margarete

Christine Helene Joseph Martina Leopoldine of Wurttem-
berg (1934–).

When it comes to polyonymous personages, can anyone
match this Roman consul of AD 169: Q. Pompeius Senecio
Roscius Murena Coelius Sextus Julius Frontinus Silius
Decianus Caius Julius [again] Eurcycles Herculeanus Lucius
Bivullus Pius Augustanus Alpinus Bellicus Sollers Julius
[yet again] Aper Ducenius Proculus Rutilianus Rufinus
Silius [again] Valens Valerius Niger Claudius Fuscus Saxa
Urytianus Sosius Priscus?

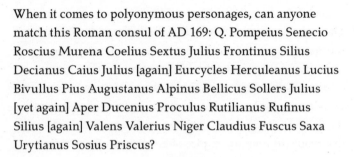

As a young publicist Scott Manning's first celebrity book
was *Eddie: My Life, My Loves,* by Eddie Fisher. According
to Scott, Fisher's brain had known better days at that point
after years of drug abuse. On *The Phil Donahue Show,*
Donahue asked him, "So you're not on drugs anymore?" to
which Eddie replied, "No." "You're sure about that?" Donahue countered.

After several intense days of squiring him around New
York, Scott was sure Eddie didn't have a clue what his name
was. "I wanted him to sign a book for me, so I decided the
polite thing to do was to remind him, 'That's Scott, with

two *t*'s.' He looked at me quizzically and signed the book. Ever the polite publicist I didn't look at it until I was alone. He had written: 'To Scott, with "two c's"--Eddie Fisher.' "

The Associated Press "Golly Martha" column titled "Under the Sea, King Resurfaces" reports that in Honolulu the humuhumunukunukuapuaa fish, known as humuhumu for short, "officially lost its title as the state fish more than a decade ago—but it's ready to reclaim the honor." Apparently, the fish was "deposed in 1990 by a clause in the original law that made the measure expire after five years." According to its sponsor, Rep. Blake Oshiro, a measure to reinstate the fish to its proud position was sparked by a six-year-old boy who wanted to know why his favorite fish no longer had an official designation.

The forty-five-letter Lake Chargoggagoggmanchauggagogg-gchaubunagungamaugg in Webster, Massachusetts, was the subject of a tune by Ethel Merman and Ray Bolger called "The Lake Song."

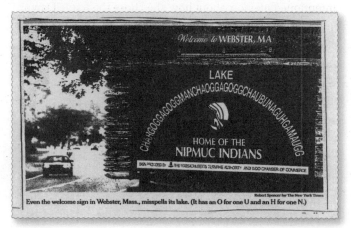

Even the welcome sign in Webster, Mass., misspells its lake. (It has an O for one U and an H for one N.)

Gordon Langley Hall was born in England, the illegitimate son of a fifteen-year-old daughter of an aristocrat (or, some say, a maidservant) and Vita Sackville-West's garage mechanic at Sissinghurst. He lived for almost thirty years as a man but in 1968, following an operation at the newly opened Gender Identity Clinic at Johns Hopkins University, he became a she and married John-Paul Simmons, a black man from Charleston, South Carolina, her newly adopted home in America. As Dawn Langley Hall Pepita Simmons I contracted for her to write a book about her sex-change operation. The manuscript she turned in was a well-intentioned memoir about how she chose the name Dawn and then added Pepita. Less than two pages were devoted to what happened at the Johns Hopkins clinic. Dame Margaret Rutherford was fascinated with Gordon/Dawn's life and was regarded by Dawn as her true "mother." After her wedding, which rocked Charleston society, *Time* magazine asked Margaret Rutherford her opinion. She replied, "Oh, I don't mind Dawn marrying a black man but I do wish she hadn't married a Baptist." The manuscript Dawn delivered to me was the basis for her autobiography, *Dawn: A Charleston Legend.*

AND THE SHORT ONES

Here's the story of the *New York Times* reporter called Jennifer 8. Lee. "Lee" is a very common surname for Chinese-Americans, and "Jennifer" is about as common whether you're Chinese or not; in fact, it was the number one girl's baby name from 1970 through 1984. Combine the two and that's a lot of Jennifer Lees. The Jennifer Lee in question was born in 1976, and, according to an article she wrote for the *Boston Globe* in 1996, she and her family decided a middle

initial was called for to differentiate herself. They settled on
8, which is good luck in Chinese culture. Ironically, she's
not the only Jenny 8 out there: Jenny 8 del Corte Hirschfeld
is a graphic designer in Manhattan who was actually christened with her numerical name. Proving, once again, it's
tough to be unique in New York.

( )

Roland Philipps and Felicity Rubinstein, London bon
vivants, named their Jack Russell terrier Dido long before
the singer with this name became famous. Incidentally,
Dido is the daughter of the late William Armstrong, a
legendary book editor at Sidgwick and Jackson in London.
I often saw Dido when she worked as an assistant to Carole
Blake, a literary agent. She once asked to leave early, saying,
"I have a gig tonight. It could be the big one." Carole and I
shared a glance, "Oh the irrepressible optimism of youth."
Carole Blake told me Dido's full name is Dido Cloud de Bou-
naville Armstrong, and that she has a brother named Rollo.

From Carole Blake, a story about a mixup of names at the
Pearly Gates.

Three Italian nuns die and go to heaven, where they are
met at the Pearly Gates by Saint Peter. He says, "Ladies, you
all led such wonderful lives that I'm granting you six months

to go back to earth and be anyone you want." The first nun says, "I want-a to be Sophia Loren" and *poof* she's gone. The second says, "I want-a to be Madonna" and *poof* she's gone. The third says, "I want-a to be Sara Pipalini." Saint Peter looks perplexed. "Who?" he says. "Sara Pipalini" replies the nun. Saint Peter shakes his head and says, "I'm sorry but that name just doesn't ring a bell." The nun then takes a newspaper out of her habit and hands it to him. He reads the paper and starts laughing. He hands it back to her and says, "No, Sister, this says 'Sahara Pipeline laid by 500 men in 7 days!'"

Simon Winchester is a splendid name, particularly for a writer of literate, original, and entertaining books on unusual historical subjects. But he wasn't always Simon Winchester. In the 1950s when he was six he was sent to a British boarding school run by the sisters of the Blessed Order of the Visitation in the town of Bridport, Dorset. The convent's rules prohibited names. Everyone was simply a number; Simon was 46. In the summertime the boys were often herded a short distance to the English Channel—the sea. Simon's first love was geology and it was here that he discovered a Jurassic fossil, an ammonite. He recounts the occasion in his 2001 book *The Map That Changed the World*.

> I gazed closely at it, enraptured by its strange deli-
> cacy.... A few of the other boys seemed interested—I

remember still that 6 and 25 in particular shared my
fascination and had asked to have a closer look.

The beast evidently left as much of an impression
on them. Many years later I came across number
25—by then he had a name and was a senior partner
in a private banking firm—while walking along Connaught Road in Hong Kong. It was during an evening
of reminiscence some while later that he asked me
if I still had that pretty little ammonite. But no, I
said shamefacedly, I didn't; and neither of us could
remember much more about the day it was found,
nor, to our greater shame, could we remember what
6, the other boy who had liked it, was really called.

When Simon Winchester read the manuscript for this book
he commented:

I can remember no pleasure comparable to browsing
the adventures of *Bertha Venation* except for the time
twenty years ago on Connaught Road in Hong Kong
when I ran into the school chum whom the nuns at
my convent school insisted on calling "Twenty-Five,"
and he embraced me with an exultant cry of "Forty-
Six!"—whereupon it took us a good five minutes to
remember what each other's name was.

He was David Paterson and he is now very rich—
and so is unlikely to apply to this delightful volume the
name of one my Australian friends: Emma Chizzit.

Eamon Dolan, former editor-in-chief of Houghton Mifflin publishers, who recently moved to The Penguin Press, is one of the funniest people I know, so it isn't surprising that he sent me a July 2000 *International Herald Tribune* clipping, "Scorer Knew the Names," that reported a game of cricket in which all twenty-two players had the same last name: Patel. "Even the scorer was called Patel when Yorkshire LPS played Amarmilan on Wednesday as Patel was caught by Patel off the bowling of Patel." The Yorkshire LPS secretary, Ishy Patel, reported that "it was the first time its starting eleven was all Patels. 'Our regular wicketkeeper who is not a Patel couldn't play and his replacement was a Patel,' he said."

Eamon worked with me for a couple of years and he was never at a loss for words. The following conversation took place with Bill Shinker, the former publisher of HarperCollins.

SHINKER: "I just learned that Anne Rivers Siddons has cut two cities out of her book tour. She can't do that. We promised Barnes and Noble she'd appear and autograph books."

DOLAN: "I know, Bill, but it has to be. Her father died and she's going back to Atlanta for the funeral."

SHINKER: "Oh." *Pause.* "Were they close?"

DOLAN (*no pause*): "Like family."

CHAPTER 5

WHAT WERE THEIR
PARENTS THINKING?:
LAUGH-OUT-LOUD FUNNY NAMES

Penelope Hoare is a distinguished editor at Chatto and Windus in London, and in fact she was recently voted Editor of the Year. She is known to one and all as Penny and is good fun to be with, especially in New York because she enthusiastically likes certain things about America. For example, good old-fashioned steaks. I make a point of taking her to dinner at Ben Benson's Steakhouse, acclaimed for its beef. On our last visit her cell phone wasn't working and, anxious about a call she was expecting, she instructed the maître d', "If anyone calls for a Penny Hoare, please let me know."

Clearly the impact that words have on us is baffling. Sound and meaning work their dual magic upon us in ways that the ear and mind alone cannot always analyze. Consider, for example, the foreign couple who decided to name their first daughter with the most beautiful English word they had ever heard.

They named the child Diarrhea.

!?!

As of November/December 2005, Jerrold Footlick was on the editorial advisory board of *Mental Floss* magazine.

Frances Ingraham Heins recalls a college friend named Hedda Lettuce.

Dulane Ponder was an editorial assistant at Doubleday in the 1960s. A Southerner, she didn't think her nickname, Dooly Ponder, was funny or unusual.

A book club manager was reviewing the list of members and found Dusty Rhodes and Treasure Hunt.

Mr. and Mrs. Cianci (pronounced See-Ann-See) named their daughter Nancy Ann.

Here's an interesting list adapted from ForteanTimes.com:

CLAIM TO FAME NAME	MEANING OF NAME
Roman emperor Caligula	A soldier's hobnobbed boot
Roman emperor Caracalla	Heavy military cloak
General Albinus	White
General Fuscus	Black
Luminary Horatius Flaccus	Big Ears
Luminary Ovidus Naso	Long Nose
Luminary Pompeius Strabo	Squint Eye

From Hilary Hale

When a friend gave birth to a baby boy, she didn't like the name Andrew, which was often used on her husband's side of the family. She did like the name Drew, however, but another friend convinced her that Drew would not be the most suitable accompaniment to the surname Peacock.

Also from Hilary Hale: Jan Snuck-Hurgronjie, the name of the guy who used to run the Naval Institute Press.

☺

From Deborah Heffernan, whose father made up stories about his friend Sally Longbottom.

We were six proper Catholic children living among the apple orchards of central Massachusetts. Sunday was a big day because we wore our best clothes and especially loved showing off our Easter bonnets (except my brother who, thankfully, didn't wear one). My father had long amused us with stories of his friend "Sally Longbottom" whose escapades distracted us from fighting with each other on excursions in the back of our Ford fake-woody station wagon. Sally had all kinds of adventures, made funnier, of course, by her impossible name. One Easter Sunday, when we were milling about outside St. Mary's church after Mass, hoping to be admired, Dad gathered us and brought us to meet a tall and elegant woman, whom he introduced as Sally Longbottom. Do you know that laughter that rears up like nausea in a child? We thought our heads would explode. Surely we must have looked contorted with gas, but we politely shook the hand the grand lady extended to each of us. She did not look like our adventuress, nor did she look like she'd find our hilarity amusing. We laughed so hard on the way home that we all had headaches and had to be put to bed. I will say this, though: she had a very long face, and long legs, but we didn't dare look at her bottom.

From Penny Price

Although my parents have always insisted that I was the one who wanted to be called "Penny" rather than "Penelope" when I was growing up, it has left me with a full name that demands to be commented upon—Penny Price. Not quite as striking as Penny Hoare, admittedly (or, perhaps, thankfully).

Penny's father worked at Ocean Group, an international shipping company, with Sue Darling, Wendy Truelove, and Roget Gotobed.

Ellen Sargent received a correspondence card with this
name at the top:

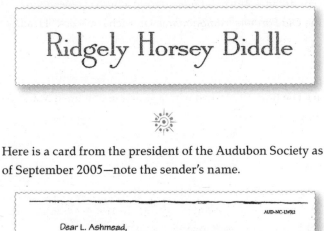

Ridgely Horsey Biddle

Here is a card from the president of the Audubon Society as
of September 2005—note the sender's name.

AUD-NC-LWR2

Dear L. Ashmead,
Please read my note inside ... it explains how
you can help protect birds that are in danger
of extinction!

John Flicker

100 Years of Conservation!

Audubon

National Audubon Society
700 Broadway • New York, NY 10003
www.audubon.org

Cover original artwork entitled *Elusive Ivory* by Larry Chandler — www.ivory-bill-woodpecker.com

From David Rosenthal, executive vice president and publisher at Simon and Schuster

For decades, the chief meteorologist of the trade edition of the *Old Farmers' Almanac* was Dr. Richard "Dick" Head.

Mary Lee Burnett worked with a young man named Mark Failing.

From Jerry Buerer

A German man is named Gottlieb Kortbein (which roughly translates to "God loves short legs").

From Theodore Butt Philip regarding himself, a story from *Liberator Magazine* (UK) titled "What's in a Name?"

The new e-mail system in Parliament, which blocks supposedly rude words, has been the subject of much mirth. It must make it hard to communicate with constituents in Cockermouth, Penistone and Scunthorpe, for example.

But now the curse of the obscenity detectors has hit the blameless Liberal Democrat federal policy committee.

The system kept rejecting its papers. The reason: the address list included Theo Butt Philip. A quick change to "Theo B-Philip" and problem solved.

⊘

From Peternelle van Arsdale, the story of Billie Grubbs.

My maternal grandmother, who was born in the very rural town of Rothville, Missouri, sometime in the second decade of the twentieth century, was named Billie Grubbs. Grubbs is truly one of the ugliest last names I've ever heard, and she has her Welsh ancestry to thank for that. She was the youngest of nine children, seven of whom survived childhood. Six of the survivors were girls. An older brother, William, aka Bill, died before she was born, and when my Mama Billie (as the grandchildren all called her) was born, her parents so hoped for a boy that they didn't even come up with a girl's name. So when she was born, yet another girl, they gave her the name of her dead brother, changing it a little to make it look like a girl's name. Hence, Billie Grubbs. To me, what's even more interesting is that when my grandmother, née Billie Grubbs, went on to have children, she gave them all beautiful names. My aunt's name is Lyle (with the accent on the "e" so it's pronounced Li-lay); my mother's name is Linda, which of course means "pretty" in Spanish; and my uncle, who is named Sor-rell (emphasis on the second syllable; it's his middle name but it's what everyone calls him), has one of the prettiest men's names I've ever heard. Who knows if her own ugly name is what led her to marry a man named Eldred Sorrell Lanier and have three children with pretty names, but it's interesting to speculate. Now, what inspired her to live in Tuscaloosa, Ala-bama, I'll never know.

From Lisa Alther, bestselling author, most recently, of *Kinfolks*

Bopeep Seahorse
Formica Dinette
Twins named Regina and Vagina
Placenta Louise

From John Marciano
An ex-girlfriend went to high school with skinny twins named Candy and Mandy Cane. Her friend from Iowa went to school with sisters Fonda Dix and Lotta Dix, star soft-ball players. When they missed a game the headline read: "Hoover High Wins with Dix Out."

From Michael Goldman

Ivor Million, with whom he attended Manchester Grammar School in the 1940s, was teased for his name, grew up to be a solicitor, stood unsuccessfully for Parliament as a Labour candidate in the 1955 General Election, and died at age fifty-four.

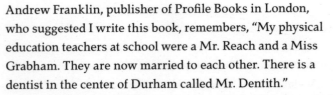

Andrew Franklin, publisher of Profile Books in London, who suggested I write this book, remembers, "My physical education teachers at school were a Mr. Reach and a Miss Grabham. They are now married to each other. There is a dentist in the center of Durham called Mr. Dentith."

Franklin has a colleague who knows of a company called Hacker Young and a graduate recruitment officer named Dimple Mystery.

He also added that there's a cookbook called *The Sex Life of Food*, authored by a Bunny Crumpacker, and that his daughter corresponds with a journalist named Jah Wobble.

April Showers was an early flute teacher of writer Dan Coffey, who left teaching to play for the Miami Symphony Orchestra.

From Patrick Walsh, a British literary agent

A girl who worked at Saatchi & Saatchi in the eighties called Venus Fish used to get annoyed because of all the fish-and-chip shops throughout South London called the "Venus Fish Bar" and was asked constantly if she owned them.

Patrick also cited a London literary agent, Sappho Clissit, adding, "whose parents should be shot."

From Catherine M. Melocik

Virginia Ham lives in Berwick, Maine, where, as her dad put it, "Hams and Beans were popular names."

Weldon Hare, pronounced "well-done hare," is an acquaintance of her grampy.

Her mother knew a Holly Woods, who was married to an IBM salesman.

Catherine also cites a Richard Head in Baltimore, but not the one who used to be an editor of *Yankee* magazine, and Czeslaw Lesiegewicz (pronounced CHEZ-law Leh-SHIZ-of-witz), an acquaintance of her father's.

Obituary, *Hudson Valley Register Star*: Zeroline I. Benschop, homemaker, schoolteacher.

A two-year-old boy is named ESPN (which his parents thankfully pronounce "Espen"). As it turns out, there are three little kids in the United States with equally obsessed parents. Not missing a beat, producers at ESPN traveled to meet each one and will feature them in an upcoming show.

Barbara Victor had a neighbor on Riverside Drive called Irving Schmuckler who changed his first name to Craig but didn't mess with Schumuckler.

Ms. Victor also knew a Pas Serieux.

A November 21, 2005, clipping from the *Weekly World News* reports a Kentucky man named Mud Larkin. "If someone says 'your name is mud,' that means you are disliked or unwanted," it reads. "So, understandably, 'Mud' is among the last choices of names parents would give to their children." But not for Daryl and Nadine Larkin. "'My daddy felt it would be character building,' explained 44-year-old trucker Mud Larkin.... 'Today, I got my own rig, own my own house—a real one, not a trailer—and I just married a pretty gal nearly half my age. Mud has been gold to me.'"

Will Swift has a friend who is a teacher on Long Island. Her name is Penny Nichols, nicknamed Dimes/Quarters. He also knows someone named Dwayne Dwopp (think "raindrop").

Spotted in *The Guardian* by Bruce Hunter: "Once we had a dinner lady called Anna Tomic. No 'bombe surprise' but her curries were always explosive!"

Bevis Hillier found in *The Spectator* (December 2004) mention of a schoolteacher named Quentin Cumber (who went by his first initial, making him Q. Cumber).

From R. L. Stine, originator of the Goosebumps books

> Sid Down
> Stan Dupp
> Ben Dover

Stine's wife, Jane, knows of a Donald Duklowitz.

Scott Manning, aka "Scooter," is amused by the names Junior Pugh of Madrid, Iowa, and Mattie Pat Pope.

Actress Donna Murphy and her husband Shawn know of a woman named Honey Zipper.

"The Big Blow by Blow," an article published in the *New York Post* (November 17, 2004), by Keith Kelly, explains that former executive editor of *George* magazine and author of *Harvard Rules* Richard Blow changed his name to Richard Bradley. Kelly reports that "After a p.r. drubbing, Blow eventually sold a completed manuscript to John Sterling and Henry Holt for an estimated $250,000. Blow insisted that is not the reason for the change. 'It's not about the controversy for "American Son,"' he said. 'I'm proud of that book... And it's not about getting teased in high school—everyone gets teased for something in high school.'"

Daisy Carrington had a piece in the *New York Observer* called "What Were Their Parents Thinking?" that cited unusual names New York parents are giving their kids these days. They include:

Geir

Mitra

Sirus (pronounced *Ziroos)*

Talia

Zosia

Zeus

Aoife

Atlas

Lachlan

Liv

Oona

Narissa

Amira

Mayher

Manelna

To name just a few.

Carrington closes the piece quoting a phone conversation with Pilar Guzman, editor in chief of *Cookie* magazine, who had trouble growing up with her name. Guzman lamented: "Even though Pilar is a relatively easy two-syllable name, you can't imagine how it was bastardized," she said. "As a kid, instead of having the instinct to say your name more loudly when you hear it mispronounced or misunderstood, your instinct is to retreat into yourself, because it's embarrassing. During those formative years, all you really want to be called is Jenny."

CHAPTER 6

DID I HEAR THAT RIGHT?:
SAY THESE NAMES
OUT LOUD AND BLUSH

When I was a graduate student at Yale in the late 1950s, Richard Foster Flint, the autocratic head of the Geology Department, decided we should have name signs minimally identifying the occupants of our tiny cubicles. L. Ashmead was fine with me; my neighbor Peter Enis was stoic but decidedly less enthusiastic.

☺

BY THE BRAND NAME
SHALL YOU KNOW THEM

Jane Friedman is the head of HarperCollins worldwide. She sets high personal and corporate goals and almost always meets them. "Brand name" is one of her personal mantras and she has had astounding success in her efforts to make HarperCollins almost universally recognized.

While brand naming can sometimes go awry it is almost always on a smaller level. During my years at Doubleday there was a large department devoted to religious books. John Delaney oversaw the division. Doubleday was an initial leader in the marketing and sales of trade paperbacks. The two biggest imprints were Barnes & Noble. (The name was sold later to the bookstore chain.) The other two were Anchor and Dolphin books, begun by Jason Epstein at Doubleday, and now they are a large division of Bertelsmann's Random House. The brand name mistake I remember had nothing to do with sales, marketing, or even the book buyers' brand name perception. It was an in-house fiasco. John Delaney wanted to start a paperback imprint aimed at the religious market. Meetings were held and everyone agreed Vision Books was close to perfect.

After a successful launch it grew into a healthy name. All was fine until it was decided to hire a new editor to head up the list. As we headed into our December sales presentations, the new editor took the podium, was introduced, and began, "Now I would like to present the new additions to Wision Books."

Our new editor had a selective speech impediment that affected only a few words. Sometimes he enunciated perfectly, sometimes not. The word he never pronounced correctly was *vision*. I don't think he was aware of this fault. At times I think he used the word and its variations more than necessary. Publishing folk are generally polite and I don't think anyone ever mentioned his impediment. A few years later he moved to another publisher where he was in charge of a line of books easily and correctly pronounced by him.

It has been increasingly common to reward book editors with a special imprint. Usually this would be the name of the editor: Nan A. Talese, Shaye Areheart, Thomas Dunne, Joanna Cotler, Marian Wood, Richard and Jeannette Seaver. No one has asked me to start an imprint, but if someone did it wouldn't be eponymous. I have a name: Miracle Books. My tagline would be irresistibly catchy: "If it is a good book it is a Miracle."

From George Costello

Dick Hartup, a psychology book author
Michael Butts, lawyer
Jay Heiny, Prentice-Hall College's director of recruitment
Jason Panty, Upper West Side burglar

I love Marmite but there is a great difference of opinion. And then there is Philadelphia scrapple. I dare you to read the list of ingredients.

FROM *Saveur* MAGAZINE

From Jeff Shapiro

Signor and Signora Melalavo (which in Italian means "I wash it")—"lo" and "la" slang for privates—named their daughter Domenica (Sunday).

☺

A Canadian teacher was presented with a computerized class list that looked something like this:

> Jones, Paul
> Smith, Bob
> Yu, Phuc

She told her Vietnamese student that Phuc was pronounced "John" in Canada and had the office change his name.

John Michel's sister went to school with a girl named Becky Fuchs, pronounced "Fewks," of course, just like the H-bomb spy Klaus. But on taking attendance that first day of seventh grade, one of the nuns at her Catholic school began, "Becky Fuh—" at which point Becky yelled out, "Fewks here!"

Novelist Kate Morgenroth reports:

> My sister used to work with a man whose name was Richard Byter—he went by the nickname Dick, Dick Byter. You have to wonder why he didn't go with Rich or something. But if that isn't bad enough, he had a son who he also named Richard Byter and who also went by Dick. And that's not all. It gets even worse. To distinguish between the two Dicks, they called the father "Big Dick Byter," and the son "Little Dick Byter." Sometimes people make you wonder, don't they?

One of my first bookseller friends was the famous Faith
Bunson, who ordered all the books for the Rich's Department Stores in Georgia. Before the advent of the megachain
bookstores, there were a few important department store
book buyers, most of them women, who could make or
break a book. Faith was powerful. She was also very funny,
especially when she told stories about her childhood in
Pearl River, Mississippi. Here's my favorite. At an early
age, Faith fell in love with one of those leather aviator caps,
complete with mock goggles and a strap. She wore it day and
night and was met everywhere with the plea, "Take it off."
For a few years she actually believed her name was "Take it
off." She liked it better than Faith.

From Carlo Grossman
    "The best real name of a person I know is Barbara
Fatt Heinie. Her father was one of the founders of Grey
Advertising, Arthur Fatt. Guess who she divorced after
marrying?"

From publicist Scott Manning
    "When I was in college I used to work summers in
a small bank in New Hampshire. Each week, a scraggly
old gentleman would come in to purchase a money order.

Whenever a new teller came on board, all the other tellers pretended to be busy when this man came in. Once, I was that new teller, and I asked him, rather innocently, for his name. 'Lester Cockburn,' he mumbled, and when I asked him to speak up the poor guy was forced to boom 'Lester Cockburn' for all the other tellers' enjoyment."

The *New York Times*, in a special supplement on India dated February 1, 2006, listed Sheila Dikshit, Delhi chief minister, who was giving a talk on "Breaking the Glass Ceiling: More Women in Top Positions."

From Farley Chase
    A Vietnamese cabdriver, female, called Phat Ho.

In his July 29, 2004, *Heckler* piece, David Hicks features a veritable laundry list of funny names: "I had some cousins called Ramsbottom who decided to change their surname to Russell," he says. "You can also understand the frustration of people called Cockburn and Mainwaring having to deal with phonetic, but incorrect, renditions of their names.

"A few months ago in North Queensland I met a 30-year-old man called Lotus. As a teenager Lotus hated his name but now he likes it—and he's straight.

"Think of all those German boys born in the 1930s called Adolf. How many were brave enough to keep their names after 1945?

"I went to school with Robert Sole. His parents had not considered the effect of his initial and his surname. (Robert Sole, R. Sole—arsehole).

"When I was a child I thought my name was all right, even if 'hicks' could also mean pimples and country bumpkins."

Murtaza from University of Chicago

"In Hinsdale Central High School's class of 2004, there was a boy named William (Bill) Bagenas."

Outspoken Yale lesbian Pam Dick has a rather remarkable masculine mother named Anita Dick.

Remarkable names of fictional characters: At the top of the list is Honeysuckle Weeks, Foyle's driver in TV's *Foyle's War,* and Hyacinth Bucket, a social hopeful in *Keeping Up Appearances*, who insists it be pronounced "Boo-Kay."

※

Simon Doonan, author of *Confessions of a Window Dresser,* is famous for his spectacularly original window displays at Barney's in New York City. He has also written a wonderful memoir, *Nasty: My Family and Other Glamorous Varmints*. He describes London when he was a young man. Many of the clubs featured drag queens. They were mostly bawdy gals who lip-synched to cassette tapes of Shirley Bassey and brayed obscenities at the audience. In the book he mentions my favorite drag name: Bertha Venation.

CHAPTER 7

༄

BY THEIR NAMES
SHALL YE KNOW THEM:
APTLY—AND ODDLY—NAMED
PROFESSIONALS

The *Columbus Ledger-Enquirer* (February 2, 2006) featured an article by Don Coker called "Name That Destiny," which shows the results of a study done by Albert Mehrabian, professor emeritus of psychology at the University of California at Los Angeles, that evaluated how naming children can affect their futures. "Children with more 'desirable' names were treated more favorably than children with less desirable names," it states, "but rules are made to be broken. Keanu, Oprah, Cher and Regis seem to have done just fine with their unusual monikers, although they probably had their share of teasing when they were children." The article also advises baby namers to consider the meaning of names. "Ms. Channing might cringe to learn that Stockard means 'from the yard of tree stumps.'" And initials? "Zachary Ian Thomas probably won't want his monogram on a tie."

☞

I moved to New York City in the early 1960s, and when I returned home for a visit I soon eagerly told my parents about the transvestites who lived openly in New York and often had colorful names. My mother smiled a bit and then said, "You know, your aunt Rhoda used to be a woman but when she graduated from high school and went to work for Kodak, she started wearing men's clothing and changed her name to Robert. We don't talk about it all the time."

Patricia Louise Thomasina Gibney sent me this bit of naming knowledge: "My mother's rule was that you always put senator in front of names being considered for a new baby—she believed this to be a surefire method of telling if the name would work and, of course, one always wanted to be prepared for the Senate."

Harriet Van Horne was a wonderful writer, perhaps best noted for her television critiques in the sadly missed *Saturday Review of Literature.* She died a few years ago and her friends gathered for a memorial service. After a series of eulogies, someone suggested taking a few moments remembering the best time each one of us had with Harriet. After a moment or two, a voice rang out. "I'm *Chlorinda.* I was Miss Van Horne's housekeeper and I can't remember even one good time I had with her. She still owes me fifty dollars and I'll be standing at the door if anyone wants to help clear up this situation." As I gave her a contribution I commented on her unusual and very appropriate name, *Chlorinda*. "Yes, I love my name, Chlorinda Bonaparte."

☺

FIVE BODY PARTS NAMED AFTER ITALIANS

Organ of Corti: the organ of hearing in the middle ear.
Alfonso Corti (1822–88) studied medicine and anatomy in Vienna and wrote a thesis on the reptilian cardiovascular system. He retired to his estates soon after publishing his work on the ear.

Eustachian tube: tube from the middle ear to the throat that equalizes pressure in the ear. Considered a father of anatomy, Bartolommeo Eustachio (c. 1520–74) worked in Rome as a physician to leading clerics.

Fallopian tubes: pair of tubes that conduct eggs from the ovaries to the uterus. Gabriel Fallopius (1523–62), a professor of anatomy at Pisa and Padua, coined the word "vagina" and invented a condom.

Ruffini's corpuscles: sensory nerve endings that respond to warmth. Angelo Ruffini (1864–1929) stained slides with gold chloride to reveal the tiny cells. Starting as a country doctor, he went on to become a professor.

Sertoli cells: cells of the testis that nourish sperm cells.

Enrico Sertoli (1842–1910) discovered them in 1865, while he was still a postgraduate student in physiology in Vienna. He later became a professor of anatomy and physiology in Milan.

From the *Book of Lists*, by David Wallechinsky and Amy Wallace.

☺

Frances Ingraham Heins, a writer who lives in Kinderhook, New York, occasionally has a weekend breakfast at the local Elks Lodge. Recently, she was served by a waitress wearing a blue plastic name card that read IDA LEISER.

Fran also contributes these interesting doctor's names from her region of Upstate New York:

> Dr. Flesh, a gynecologist
> Dr. Wolf and Dr. Lamb, both vets
> Dr. Chew, another vet
> Dr. Finger, a foot doctor

☺

From Mark Lawless

Ms. Zee Cabbagestalk, adjuster, Crawford and Company
Laura Porko, group merchandising manager at Amazon
I also heard from Marion Lear Swaybill, who notes that

Damon L. Cabbagestalk ran for New York City public advocate in the 2005 primary.

Barbara Moulton, now a literary agent in San Francisco, sent me her favorite family name story, pointing out that "I am a twelfth-generation native of the Pine Tree State (Maine). My grandfather was named James Forrest Moulton. He had three brothers, but the only one left in my lifetime was Woodbury Harold Moulton. The brothers lived in the same small town of Kennebunk their entire lives. Grampa was always known as Forrest, and Woodbury as Woody. Woody drove the only cab in town, and Forrest had the only remaining dairy farm that sold milk to customers. So Woody and Forrest hail from the Pine Tree State. I called my dad to get Woody's full name, and he had never noticed the Forrest-Woody thing until I mentioned it."

Michael Pollan is a fine writer of essays, articles, and books (most notably *The Botany of Desire* and *Second Nature*). He also collects what he refers to as aptonyms, a word not in my dictionary, but from the list he shared with me his search is for names that reflect a profession. Here is a hilarious selection (with additional contributions from Ruth Katz, Karen Hochman, and Laura Bellon).

Dr. Anil Ram, gastroenterologist

Dr. Butt, gastroenterologist

Karmen Butterer, byline on a quote about a high-fat foods and overeating study in *Health* magazine

Rebecca Weiner, Weimaraner Club of America's breed-rescue coordinator

Dante Swallow, six-year-old boy bitten by a mountain lion

Dr. Robert Stuffs, physician sued for "botched, painful penile-lengthening surgery"

Janet Woodcock, FDA spokesperson answering inquiries about Viagra

Oliver Saucy, chef

Lieutenant Greg Bone, Berkeley, California, police officer who signed in American Indian artifacts unearthed during road work, including one full skeleton and parts of four or five others

Larry Tiller, vegetable merchant at San Francisco's Ferry Plaza Market

Shawn Roe, fishmonger at Seattle's Pike Place Market

Mr. Hung T. Dong, leader of an organized crime family that controls prostitution in southern California

Michelle Passoff, author of *Lighten Up! Free Yourself from Clutter*

John Broadwater, spokesperson for the Monitor National Marine Sanctuary

Roy Blomquist (pronounced "Bloomquist"), chief horti-culturist, city of Boston

Tom Thunder, acoustical engineer

James Goodness, spokesman for the Newark, New Jersey, archdiocese

John Perry Fish, American Underwater Search and Survey

Lieutenant Ron Nipper, spokesman for a California prison, quoted in an article about curtailing the production of Pruno, an alcoholic beverage surreptitiously made by prisoners from just about anything

Lance Lalumiere, firefighter convicted of arson

Simon Rattle, music director, Britain's City of Birmingham Symphony Orchestra

Hugh Fish, British environmental engineer whose love of pristine rivers helped clean up the Thames

Larry Hawk, D.V.M., president and CEO of the ASPCA

Lieutenant Sid Heal, nonlethal weaponry authority, Los Angeles

Johnnie Worm, California peach grower

Dr. Shelly Hoover, diet doctor

Tyrone Killingsworth, murderer

Andrew Inches, videotape editor, WABC-TV

Seth Kugel, byline on an article in the *New York Times* about a tortilla maker

Mr. Rusty Cockman, a Clover, South Carolina, planning commissioner charged with lewd behavior

Karen Kaeffer, Kellogg's "Special K" spokesperson

Julian Senior, senior vice president, European marketing, Warner Bros.

Bruno Jamais, maître d' at Restaurant Daniel

Laurent Gras, chef

Also from Michael Pollan comes the official "Doctor's Names List," collected from the Medical Libraries Discussion List.

Dr. Brain, neurologist

Dr. Leash, Dr. Barker, Dr. Wagy: veterinarians

Rita Book, medical librarian

Billie Odor, certified colon hydrotherapist

Dr. Polymeropolous, research specialist in polymorphism

Dr. Seymour Landa, optometrist

Dr. Slaughter, Dr. Kutteroff, Dr. Hacker, Dr. Butcher: surgeons

Dr. Bones, chiropractor

Dr. Butcher, Dr. Harm, Dr. Hurter, Dr. Toothaker, Dr. Root, Dr. Nasti, Dr. Paine: dentists

Dr. Pitts, Dr. Skinner, Dr. Whitehead: dermatologists

Dr. Grab, Dr. Catching, Dr. Gass, Dr. Handwerker, Dr. Born, Dr. Hatcher, Dr. Hooker, Dr. Finger, Dr. Cocks, Dr. Nippel: OB/Gyns

Dr. Broth, oncologist

Dr. Dick, Dr. Spear, Dr. Tapper, Dr. Waters, Dr. Splatt: urologists

Dr. Bunny, Dr. Tickles, Dr. Sno White: pediatricians

Dr. Looney, Dr. Crabb: psychiatrists

Dr. Albright, Dr. Vu: radiologists

Dr. Nalebuff, hand surgeon

Dr. Cure, Dr. Gore: emergency medicine

Dr. Breidin, respiratory

Dr. Safety R. First, cardiologist

Dr. Bonebrake, pulmonary medicine

Dr. Strange, mental health director

Dr. Kidd, pediatrician

Dr. Foote, Dr. Cornfield, Dr. Shoemaker, Dr. Smellsey, Dr. Tozzi, Dr. Footer: podiatrists

Plus

Dr. Neil Gesundheit

Dr. Wolf, D.V.M.

From R. Sonn, Somerset County, New Jersey

A dentist named Dr. Pullen

A veterinarian named Dr. Qwaak

A construction company called Terrible Construction Company, probably based on the Italian family name Terribile

Janet Whaley, the national stranded mammal coordinator

From David Tripp

Winston Churchill's neurologist was named Russell First Baron Brain. David wonders if there is a Second.

Emma Sweeney, a friend and fellow literary agent, reports
on a Texas legend.

Even in death, Candy Barr, the 1950s stripper who
became the most infamous, loved, and loathed woman in
Texas, still fascinates and titillates. *Texas Monthly* executive
editor Skip Hollandsworth held a crowd at Julia Sweeney's
Talk Series at the Park City Club in rapt attention with his
narrative of how Candy's show business career was almost
launched at the age of sixteen when she played the spoons
on *The Ted Mack Amateur Hour*. When lucrative spoon
gigs didn't materialize she went from runaway to teenage
porn star, Dallas burlesque queen, mafia moll, famed prison
convict, and, finally, a quiet death in a south Texas hospital
at age seventy.

Despite being used and abused, Candy (née Juanita
Slusher) never lost her little-girl appeal or her big-girl sass.
Colony Club owner Abe Weinstein baled her out of jail in
1956 after she shot and wounded her husband when he
came home drunk and abusive. (After hearing Candy's side,
a grand jury declined to indict.) At her post-bail news conference, Candy looked at the photographers and said, "Make
it sexy, boys."

David Tripp, crediting Leslie Meredith, his editor at The
Free Press: "I knew a guy in the army reserves named Larry
Light. He went on to become a lieutenant colonel, a rank

usually referred to as 'light colonel,' which made him Light Colonel Light."

From Susan Scopetta, wife of fire commissioner Nick Scopetta: Dr. Sheldon Cherry, an OB/Gyn at Columbia Presbyterian, penned a number of books on "feminine hygiene."

From Tim Hely Hutchinson
   A dentist named Dr. Fang
   A chief instructor at a San Francisco gym called Randy Hamburger

PHOTO: TAD HODDICK

From Neal Terman

> Derek K. S. Bigrigg, deceased violinist
>
> Rehema Ellis, reporter
>
> Harry Kramp, high school swim coach
>
> Harry Strum, high school guitar teacher

A store in Noosa that sells boxer shorts is called Strictly Ballooom.

A septic company in New Zealand is called Macdonald's Takeaways (talk about brand names!).

Sherry Suib Cohen knows a Westport law firm called Slez and Slez and a New York City law partnership named Lawless and Lynch.

Bruce Hunter, a noted London literary agent, spotted an American law firm named Amend & Amend and one in Hobart, Austrialia, called White and Wong.

Bruce's longtime friend Belinda Hollyer noted in *The Guardian*: "The Howard League for Penal Reform is directed by an F. Crook, also there's a medical specialist named C. Burns-Cox and when Stewart Collins applied for a job as a road safety officer, he was interviewed by a Mr. Carr and a Mr. Rhodes."

Susan Fletcher, a book publisher in London, has an eye for apt names: Helena Reckless, a surgeon; Noble Power, Canadian ambassador; and Mr. Fatty, the head of the Freedom from Hunger Campaign.

Cynthia Hart noted that in one of the many Disney legal battles reported by Dominick Dunne in *Vanity Fair* the chief of security at the Chancery Court, who controls the operations of the place, is a no-nonsense former state trooper named, appropriately, Rocky Justice. He was named for Rocky Lane, his father's favorite cowboy movie star in the 1930s. Admired by all, Justice keeps everything in order, gives out the press passes each day, pats you down if the alarm goes off on the security system, and tells the people in the courtroom to stand up for Judge Chandler's entries and exits.

Charles Spissu reported: "In the early 1980s I worked for a manufacturer of textiles and there I met two elderly ladies who worked in the main finishing department where various chemicals were applied to cloth for apparel. Their names were Polly and Esther."

Two corporate heads of engineering at Lorillard Tobacco had the surnames Block and Head. They were known to their office buddies as "the Blockhead Brothers."

The following are from Mark Lawless.

Fritz Funfrock, pastry chef

Douglas N. Daft, chairman and CEO of Coca-Cola

Rich Guy, head of marketing for Blue Zemu Gel

Preetinder S. Bharara, lawyer

Richard M. Moneymaker, Los Angeles attorney

Michael W. Popoff, Beverly Hills criminal attorney

Jonny Kool, lawyer

John Raymond Gonzo, lawyer

Dr. Wizwell, urologist

Ross F. Schmucki, attorney

Virginia Dingleberry, claimant on a lawsuit

Wong Wee Woo, managing director for Pearson Southeast Asia

Googoosh, an Iranian singer

David Youngstrom, a former sales rep for HarperCollins, had a meeting with this personal banker in New Jersey:

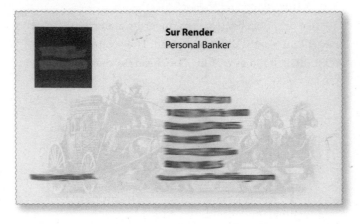

Sur Render
Personal Banker

Craig Young relates that his boss spent a great deal of time in discos in downtown Manhattan in the 1970s and '80s and loved the names of the drag queens who performed there. Three that really stick out for him are Patty O'Furniture, Ida Slapter, and Iona Trailer.

Marjorie M. Nutt is the classified ads manager for *Dartmouth Alumni Magazine*. (This is one of many magazines where I ran ISO classified ads hoping for responses to be used in this book. My British publisher thought this was foolish. "A funny

name is a one-night-stand ad, not a long term relationship."
He was right but it wasn't a total waste of money.)

This satirical send-up of the bestselling novel *God of Small Things* by Arundhati Roy is peripheral to the main focus of this book but the four-star humor gets it in under the wire. It was first published in the *Literary Review* and reprinted in *Private Eye*.

I shall start at the beginning. Or near the beginning. Perhaps a little after the beginning, then I'll go back to the real beginning, after which I can skip you forwards again to the not-beginning that I began with. I know—I'll start by spending a lot of time telling you where I'm going to begin. That's a good idea. I used to use this technique when I was twelve and found it hard to fill up a whole page of my exercise book. When I was twelve, I also met a sweet-seller who made me touch him in funny places. But that's another story.

So. The beginning. This is easy. I've done more than a hundred words already. Writing a novel isn't going to take me very long at all.

At the beginning a white man arrived on my doorstep in New Delhi. "I want to be your literary agent," he said. "I am the God of Large Cheques, and I would like to sell your novel all over the world."

"I haven't written a novel." I said.

"Oh bollocks," he replied. "I've lost the bit of paper with the address on it. Someone round here has written a novel."

"Come in, maybe I can help." I replied, utterly implausibly, but knowing on instinct that this would be a clever way to lurch the plot forward seamlessly.

"What is that delicious smell?" he exclaimed, passing my threshold and bumping into Ammu, my obligatory bossy Indian mother.

"Ah, it's a pudding I'm baking." I replied.

"It smells extraordinary!"

"Well—it has a unique twist. I follow an ordinary recipe, but I ever-so-subtly multiply the number of eggs by ten."

"Genius!" he exclaimed, the words bursting from his mouth like an over-ripe mango exploding in the midday sun of the hottest Keralan summer since that awful year of the fateful election victory by the hateful communists who are more corrupt than an over-ripe mango exploding in the midday sun.

"Oh, it's only a small thing," I replied.

"Allow me to explain my problem," he uttered. "I need a novel set in India. Something completely fresh and original. Something that's never been done before. A kind of fifth rate imitation of *Midnight's Children*, but written by a photogenic woman and set in a slightly different part of the country."

"There must be a novel somewhere in the house that we can sell you," said Ammu. "I'll go upstairs and look for a manuscript."

"Novels don't just grow on trees, you know, Ammu," I said sternly.

The white man gasped. "Your turn of phrase! It's so immaculate, fresh and interesting. Maybe you can do it! Maybe you can write the novel!"

"Not possible," I replied. "I have only a minimal command of English."

"That's perfect!" he blurted. "We can start now."

"But how shall I do it?"

"It's easy. The first thing to know is that you must forget all rules of readability and sentence structure, and use any trick of punctuation—anything at all—to make your sentences long; as long as you can—allowing them to run on indefinitely: they can even bleed into one another altogether so you have to go back and read the sentence again which everyone these days takes as a sign of good style. Then, when you're ready. You use short ones. For jokes. When there's something funny. Short sentences. For your jokes. For labouring jokes. Labouring them. The. Jokes."

"I'm not sure I understand."

"It's easy. Look—did you ever watch *Mind Your Language*? Use the Indian character in that as a basis. Keep everyone quaint and make them talk funny. It sells by the bucket load. And throw in a few wise

old aunts. And a pickle factory. That's compulsory.
Doesn't your mother work in a pickle factory?"

"No. She's a civil servant."

"What's wrong with you? Why doesn't your
mother work in a pickle factory? India's a spicy,
brightly-coloured country, so everyone works in
pickle factories."

"She's a civil servant. She's always been a civil
servant."

"And stop talking like that!"

"Like what?"

"Like that! With all your words separate. You're
supposed to be Indian. Sotalk likethis. Join your
wordsup. Don'tyouknow anything? Didn't you *ever*
watch *Mind Your Language*?"

"I've never heard of it."

"And what's wrong with this room? It's so drab.
Where are all your brightly-coloured drapes and
funny ethnic statues?"

"What are you talking about? This is the nineties."

"Oh, it's tragic what's happened to the scenic
countries of the world. You'll have to set your novel in
the past. We need colour, ethnic nik-naks, and prefer-
ably a sweet-seller who interfered with you when you
were a little girl. A bit of sexual abuse is compulsory
if you want to be taken seriously."

"She'll do it," said Ammu, bursting into the
room.

"But how did you hear our conversation? You were upstairs," I said.

"Oh stop being so fussy," said the God of Large Cheques. "You'll never get a novel finished if you waste your time worrying about stupid things like that."

"Get out of my house," shouted Ammu bossily, serving her usual function of finishing scenes with handy rapidity. "My daughter has a novel to write."

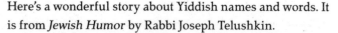

Here's a wonderful story about Yiddish names and words. It is from *Jewish Humor* by Rabbi Joseph Telushkin.

American-Jewish sex jokes often turn on Yiddish words that are "dirty"; indeed, a disproportionate number of the few Yiddish words most American Jews know are vulgar, most notably *shmuck* and *putz*. *Shmuck* derives from a German word meaning "jewel"; in a burst of either sexual self-confidence or irony, Jews appropriated this word to refer to the penis. I've always felt sympathy for people named Shmuckler, which is more or less the Yiddish equivalent of "Prickman." The *San Francisco Chronicle* (August 28, 1987) reported a little-known episode from the Iran/Contra hearings. A Lieutenant Colonel Robert Earl testified before the congressional committee that the originator of the plan to help the contras was a "General Buck Shmuck."

"That's a real name?" asked chief counsel Arthur Liman. Assured by Earl that it was, Liman, who knows some Yiddish, commented: "The only guy who should have used a code name in this case didn't." The Pentagon subsequently stated that there was no General Buck Shmuck on active duty.

Rabbi Telushkin also relates that the conservative columnist William F. Buckley once received a very abusive letter from a Dr. Prickman, to which he responded: "My friends call me Buck. What do your friends call you?"

:)

On Wednesday, **July 27, 2005**, between 4:30 and 6:30 p.m., please join us at the Albany Pump Station and help us say goodbye to **PAUL ORGAN** as he prepares to leave State Service and move into his retirement home

COURTESY OF TAD HODDICK

My longtime favorite restaurant in New York City is Michael's, owned by Michael McCarty. He is ably assisted by the always welcoming and genial Steve Millington. I hold a dubious attendance record at Michael's. On one day I went there for breakfast, lunch, drinks, and dinner—all with different people. At closing time Michael suggested he bring out a rollaway bed.

The real genius behind Michael's, however, is Loréal Sherman, the maître d'. I asked her how it is that she shares

her name with the worldwide famous company, makers
of beauty products. "Claudia, my mother, was a beautician
in Minnesota when they introduced L'Oréal in America,
and she loved the name so much she just knew if she had
a daughter..." She did and she was named Loréal Steiner.
Loréal went to schools in Minnesota, then Concordia
University and drama school in New York. She is an accomplished singer with rave notices from critics and applause
from the public but that doesn't always pay the bills. She
joined Michael's fourteen years ago. I liked her from the
start, especially because she loves to read and loved to hear
stories her husband Aaron Sherman read to her when she
was pregnant. Someday the child will read *Bel Canto* by
Ann Patchett and say to herself, "I have already read this!"
Loréal and Aaron now have a daughter, Sophia Grace-Hazel,
and she is as beautiful as her mother.

Anyone named Swatch? Literary agent John Michel remembers two interesting names derived from watches. Elgin
Baylor, the legendary basketball player of the 1960s, was
so named because when he was born his father looked at
his pocket watch to determine the time of birth—an Elgin.
Similarly, a relative of John's worked at an inner-city YMCA
one summer where he met Speidel Monday: his father also
looked at his watch and noticed the Speidel wristband.

CHAPTER 8

⤖

WHEN SO-AND-SO MARRIED SO-AND-SO: THE PRODUCTS OF FUNNY NAME UNIONS

Here's a contribution from friend Betsy Nolan (whose brother-in-law is Harry Kunze).

Bill Leak, a columnist for the *Australian*, grew up with a neighbor named Kate Savage. Having put up with that for her first twenty-five years, she married Keith Slaughter.

Hal Swetnam worked with a woman named Gay for more than a year. She had an ordinary surname from her first husband, but a year or so after her divorce she married a man named Billie Beach, which made her Gay Beach.

A literary agent, Janis Donnaud, had childhood friends named Barbara Fatt and Bill Heavy. They got married. Odd names before the union, odder after, and odder still when they had twin boys, Lemon Jello and Orange Jello.

Marriage announcements from Bill Harris:

Cockman-Dickman
Mustard-Pickels
Fillinger-Goode
MacDonald-Berger
Wendt-Adaway
Filler-Quick
Dunnam-Favors
Drinkwine-Layer
Gowen-Geter
Weener-Whipple
Peters-Rising
Butts-McCracken
Kuntz-Dick
Aikin-Johnson
Busch-Graber
Fears-Johnson
Pullen-Wood
Wacker-Daily

Author Andrew Solomon's father went to law school with Mel Hiney, who married a Smith classmate of her mother's called Barbara Fatt, and became Barbara Fatt Hiney.*

His mother's friend Sandra Caplan married James Schor and became Sandy Shor.

His college classmate had a high school teacher with the first name of Vermester, who married Mr. Bester and became Vermester Bester.

Llonald King sent me this note: "Joseph Cotten's son married (against his family's wishes) the girl next door. Her name was Velvet Satin, Satin being a name the father of the family, who was an immigrant from eastern Europe, had adopted and made legal. Thus the young woman's name became Velvet Satin Cotten. My first wife was a sorority sister of Velvet Satin at USC in the 1960s."

From Dan Coffey

Niece Rachel Coffey married a man with the last name Bean and became Rachel Coffey-Bean.

---

* In an earlier entry the last name is Heinie; on the preceding page it is Heavy. No version is in the Manhattan telephone book; all three are funny.

Jay Grelen, a reporter in Little Rock, has a flair for writing both fiction and nonfiction. He has an inquisitive eye and found every one of the words below at least once as a last name when he searched www.switchboard.com.

Belly	Bone	Toe
Dimple	Liver	Finger
Nerve	Kidney	Gland
Cheek	Head	Heel
Vessel	Foot	Ankle
Blood	Arm	Knuckle
Nose	Tongue	Lung
Tonsil	Taste	Ear
Neck	Chest	Elbow
Tooth	Breast	Knee
Teeth	Hip	Eye
Voice	Gut	Hair
Backbone	Knee	Spine
Spine	Hiney	Artery
Wrist	Butt	Flesh
Ovary (O'Vary)	Brain	Skin
Sight	Gland	Stomach
Lip	Leg	Smile
Lips	Vein	Vocal
Heart	Cornea	Jaw

Steve Fischer is a longtime sales rep for book publishers and is now executive director of the New England Independent Booksellers Association. He had a friend in college, Rhea Goldbert, who married Jonathan Poister. In a time when very few women were taking their husband's family names, Rhea did—and became Rhea Poister.

From a British newspaper:

"Lady Sophia Herbert, eldest daughter of the Earl of Pembroke, was married on Saturday at the Church of St Mary and St Nicholas in Wilton. Her groom, Alexander Murray Threipland, is the eldest son of Wyndham Murray Threipland.... [Lady Sophia's] mother, who is Lord Pembroke's first wife, Claire, is now married to Wyndham Murray Threipland."

CHAPTER 9

∽

THAT'S *PHYDEUX* TO YOU!:
FUNNY NAMES
BESTOWED UPON PETS

I've had cats most of my life and I can't imagine life without
at least one, often more. My darkest days are when a cat
dies and I wonder why I keep giving my heart to a relatively
short-lived animal. Of course, cat lovers know why. I would
spend days thinking up original and clever names for my
new cats—Hildegard, Bodley, Trapdoor, Newton, etc. Then
I decided on a simple plan and named them after the street
or road where they were born. Most of them had a good life
and plenty of it. When they died I had them cremated and
put their remains in black-painted medium-sized instant
coffee jars and lined them up on sunny windowsills. As I
write this I can see a row labeled Maple, Lexington, Fithian,
America (born on Manhattan's Sixth Avenue, officially
known as Avenue of the Americas). Fond memories. Cats!
I love them, I love books about them, and I've published
many of them. One day Ed Burlingame, publisher at Lippin-
cott, decided enough was enough. "No more cat books! The

market is overcrowded and there are better ways to spend your time." I bared my claws. "Ed, the problem is you really don't like cats!" "That's not true, Larry, I think we even have a cat at home."

I now live with a beautiful Abyssinian named Isaac and a handsome golden retriever, Tobin. I've had a series of Abyssinians, all of them superintelligent and people friendly. The Isaac now in residence has a thirdhand name. When I got my first Abyssinian I didn't follow my street-where-you-were-born rule. Because he was exceptionally alert, energetic, and smart, I named him after Isaac Asimov (about a year later I discovered they shared a birthday, January 2). The first Isaac died after a long and happy life as did the second. When the third arrived (a Fourth of July birthday present from my partner Walter Mathews), he was a kitten duplicate of the first. He is a fine memorial to Isaac, a good friend and fine writer.

I chose "Tobin" because it was the maiden name of Mary Hedges, the "temptress" I mentioned in chapter 1. She loved golden retrievers and always had a pair at her side. Tobin and Isaac are constant companions. Their hair is a beautiful red and a perfect match. When the late Lucille Ball once mentioned she always matched her poodles' fur color to her hair color (which perfectly matched the color of the Lucille Ball Rose) someone suggested that perhaps I had matched the colors of my cat and dog. Not true; it is one of God's small gifts. Lucille Ball also mentioned in the same interview that her husband, Gary, made sure she wouldn't have to suffer seeing her beloved toy poodles get old and die. At just the right time, Gary would find a home for the current dog and bring home a younger replacement, fur already dyed the perfect color. Ms. Ball intimated she knew about the switches and now and then she would run into people walking a poodle with a distinctive orange fur and a yap of recognition.

Dogs are relatively new in my life. When I was seven I loved my Beagle Yorky and was griefstricken when he was run over and killed by a Dairylea milk delivery truck. On the spot I took a solemn oath that I would never drink milk again and I haven't. I also said I would never have another dog, and would just live with my memories of Yorky. Sixty-odd years later I broke that pledge and I'm glad I did. So is Tobin.

Years later I published a diet book, *It's Not Your Fault You're Fat,* and always needing to lose weight I tried the diet. I was doing pretty good but on a trip to Rochester I had a candy binge. (It seemed justified at the time because Rochester was the birthplace of Fanny Farmer.) An aunt saw me cramming the caramels and commented, "You know, it's too bad that milk truck wasn't a candy truck."

Fred Gettings in his *The Secret Lore of the Cat* follows up on the idea that a cat should have at least two names.

There is more than a poetic fancy in the idea that a cat should have at least two names—one which is the name of the outer cat, and one which is the secret name of its inner being. T. S. Eliot's *Old Possum's Book of Practical Cats* has gained much fame in recent years through the stage version *Cats*, even though a few of the esoteric references in the poems appear to have been missed in the production. In the poem "The Naming of Cats" Eliot muses on the notion that cats have three names, the last of which is one "that no human research can discover"—the one which the cat alone knows. Eliot plays with the fancy that when a cat is in a state of profound meditation, it is actually engaged in the contemplation of its true name, like a fakir or Buddhist rapt in meditation of the powers beyond the navel. According to this poem, then, there are three names: there is the ordinary name, the personalized name and the "deep and inscrutable singular Name." How do these correspond to the occult tradition, with which Eliot was so familiar?

The ordinary name "that the family uses daily" is fairly obvious—this is the "world name" by which the cat is identified on the material plane. Yet there is a second name, also known to humans, which is more "peculiar, and more dignified." This is the name which allows the cat to keep its tail perpendicular and to spread out its whiskers and cherish its pride. Eliot gives some amusing versions of these names, such as Munkustrap and Jellyorum, but I suppose that "Pyewacket" is such a name, and perhaps one of the most famous cat names of this order is "Foss," used by the great nineteenth-century humorist Edward Lear for his own feline companion.

The distinction between the first and second names of the cat is not really all that obvious. We may not find it easy to distinguish between the two forms unless we have some understanding of an occult theosophical teaching with which Eliot was familiar, for the poet is actually referring to a genuine occult notion. The second name, which keeps the cat's tail perpendicular (pointing to heaven) corresponds to a special state of animal development recognized by occultists and called "individualization."

According to a piece in the *New York Post* on Monday, November 7, 2005, "Fido is no longer a chic name for a dog. An up-market Fido is now named Phydeux."

Heidi Singer, in her "Reigning Cats' and Dogs' Names Get Personal" (*New York Post,* November 7, 2005) article, says, "Americans are giving their pets human names, such as Jack, Chloe, and Simon." The piece quotes Betsy Saul, president of Petfinder.com, who says, "For real pet lovers, a pet is just another member of the family, so a human name seems totally appropriate." Also quoted is psychotherapist Dr. Wallace Sife, saying, "A Fido or a Fluffy is more for the family who has a cute pet … If it's a real member of the family, it will probably get a people name."

Top tags

Favorite names for dogs

MALE	FEMALE
1. Buddy	1. Daisy
2. Max	2. Molly
3. Jake	3. Sadie

Favorite names for cats

MALE	FEMALE
1. Smokey	1. Molly
2. Max	2. Angel
3. Charlie	3. Lucy

Source: Petfinder.com

FROM THE *NEW YORK POST*

Peter Carson, longtime stalwart of British publishing, is now at Profile Books. He is always interested in the arcane and wanted to be sure I knew that.

"Chekhov's two dachshunds were called Bromide (male) and Quinine (female)—in Russian and in full: Brom Isayevich and Kina Markonva."

A parakeet was named Onan because he spilled his seed on the ground.

Scott Manning tells me that the late Sidney Sheldon and his wife had two perfectly coiffed bichons frises called Monet and Renoir. Kathy Lee Gifford's dogs of the same breed: Chablis and Chardonnay.

Cindy Adams loves Yorkies. Her first was Jazzy, and she now has Jazzy Jr. and Juicy. She is one of the great gossip columnists, at least when she's nice, which is most of the time. I remember her column that appeared the day after Liberace died; it began with a memorable line: "How does one type a tear?" I shared her love of Liberace and was fortunate enough to edit his last book, *The Wonderful Private World of Liberace*. At our first meeting I urged him to give the reader some new and noteworthy anecdotes that would get off-the-book-page attention. When the manuscript was delivered he said, "There are two great stories here. One is a very funny account of a dinner party where I cooked my famous lasagna. I'd had a few drinks and when I grabbed the grated Parmesan cheese container with the bright green label I got the Comet cleaner by mistake! Boy, what a sensation at the table." And? "For the first time I tell every-one how I invented Popcorn Chenille!"

Both Hilary Spurling, author most recently of a two-volume life of Matisse, and Hilary Hale, editor extraordinaire of Macmillan in London, inform me Marie Laurencin has named her cat Poussiquette. (Hilary also remembers a little girl in the Hotwells district of Bristol who said on her first day of nursery school that she was called "Psish." When asked to spell it, her mother told them P-S-Y-C-H-E.)

!

ANIMAL REPORT, CAN EWE BELIEVE IT?

From Joelle Yudin, a former editor and always an animal lover.

A sheep saved her own life this week with a brave escape from a slaughterhouse on a Welsh farm. Myfanwy the ewe leapt into a lake and swam nearly one hundred feet to an island, where she lived on only daffodils for six weeks. Farmer Philip Robinson managed to find her and bring the eight-year-old ewe to his farm. He has decided to keep her as a pet. Robinson has six hundred ewes on his farm. .

A contribution from Richard S. Klotz of Brooklyn: an excerpt from "Jubilate Agno" (c. 1762) by Christopher Smart.

> For I have a providential acquaintance with men who bear the name of animals.
> For I bless God to Mr. Lion, Mr. Cock, Mr. Cat, Mr. Talbot, Mr. Hart, Mrs. Fysh, Mr. Grubb and Miss Lamb.
> For I bless God for the immortal soul of Mr. Pigg of Downham in Norfolk.

Stuart Proffitt, of Penguin Books in London: Sir Roy Strong's cat is named the Reverend Wenceslas Muff and is now commemorated in his garden.

Patrick Walsh spotted an Alsatian dog in Hyde Park called Puss, "whose owner claimed the name was post-ironic."

From my editor Hugh Van Dusen comes an excerpt on Churchill's pets at Chartwell. It's from the second volume of Manchester's biography.

> Should his visitors include a guest of great eminence, Churchill will offer to show him round Chartwell's

grounds. Otherwise, he proceeds with his first afternoon activity: feeding his golden orfe, ducks, and swans. Donning a Stetson—if there is a chill in the air, he will also wear an overcoat—he heads for a broad wicker chair beside the goldfish pond, calling ahead, "Arf! Arf" or "Yoick! Yoick!"

They rush to greet him, though a servant, a step behind him, has what they want. Twice a month Frank Jenner collects a blue baby-food tin at the local railway station. Within, packed in sawdust, are maggots, the caviar of goldfish gourmets. Winston offers a lidful of maggots to the fish; when it is empty he holds out the lid to be refilled. Nearby a wooden box contains bread crumbs. These Churchill feeds to the ducks and swans.

His interest in all creatures on his estate is unflagging. As a young Colonial Office under secretary he had been an enthusiastic hunter of wild game, but those days are past. Now he holds a kitten to his face and murmurs, "Darling." It is true that he kicked a large tabby cat that played with the telephone cord when he was speaking to the lord chancellor of England, shouting, "Get off the line, you fool!"—and hastily telling the chancellor, "Not you!" But afterward he offered the cat his apologies, which he never extends to human beings, cajoling the pet, cooing, "Don't you love me anymore?" and proudly telling his valet at breakfast next day, "My Mickey came to see me this morning. All is forgiven."

From a letter to Winston from Clementine, dated August 31, 1929, when the statesman was touring the United States: "Major Morton dined with us & helped keep in countenance Mr. Lennox Boyd who was surrounded by a cloder of (6) cats."

In the May 5, 2007, *New York Post,* Sam Blake Hofstetter explains why horses are named the way they are. The rules are very strict. Names can be no more than eighteen characters, no duplicate names, no popular names, no endings in "filly," "colt," "stud," "mare," or "stallion." Hofstetter gives some hilarious examples:

Curlin
Imawildandcrazyguy
Breakwind out of Warm Breeze
Victory Smile out of Fluoride, who was owned by a dentist
Lewinsky out of Dangerous Lady
Page Six
Page Six Obsessed

The following article, "Queen Victoria and 'those four-footed friends no bribe can buy,'" by Paul Johnson about Queen Victoria's household pets appeared in *The Spectator*:

An account of the recent excavations of the royal zoo at the Tower of London suggests that English monarchs took delight in baiting wild animals. I rather doubt it. Fondness of English royalty for animals goes back a long way, though it did not arouse comment before the early 19th century. Queen Victoria set the tone. She formed passionate attachments to animals when a child, and the vehemence with which she fought for their rights persisted to the end. At her various jubilees prisoners were released all over the empire provided that she personally signed their remission. There was only one category she refused: those convicted of cruelty to animals, which she called 'one of the worse traits in human nature'.

I have just been going through the sumptuous two-volume catalogue of Victorian pictures in the royal collection, edited by Oliver Millar. I had to pay a hefty sum for it, but it is now out of stock and will never be reprinted. It is full of interest, containing all Victoria's own purchases, with annotations on when and how and why they were made, and what she paid. Pictures of her dogs form a distinct and appealing group. She employed various minor artists, such as George Morley, T.M. Joy and F.W. Keyl, who might receive as little as £10 for what she called a 'doggie picture'. The best of them is Charles Burton Barber's brilliant portrait of Marco, a favourite spitz, who was actually allowed to jump on the Queen's breakfast table, where Barber shows him disporting. But the Queen's favourite dog painter was, naturally, Landseer, who was paid 50 to 150 guineas, sometimes more. When she first employed him he was, she recorded, 'an unassuming, pleasing and very young-looking man, with fair hair', and she saw him through all his vicissitudes until he died insane in 1873. If Victoria liked someone, she tolerated all their faults, in Landseer's case intemperance, swearing, dilatoriness and flagrant adultery with the Duchess of Bedford in idyllic Glen Feshie.

In return Landseer gave his best. He first won her heart with a beautiful picture of her King Charles spaniel, Dash. It was given to her, as a young teenager in 1833, by Sir John Conroy, the *éminence grise* of her awful mother. He hoped thereby to appease her feelings of hatred towards him, of which he was aware. The ploy did not work, but dog and princess became inseparable, Dash spending 'his little life' in her room. She dressed him in scarlet jacket and blue trousers, and at Christmas she gave him three india-rubber balls and two bits of gingerbread decorated

with holly and candles. Victoria had him painted half
a dozen times at least, sometimes with other dogs
such as the greyhound Nero and the huge mastiff
Hector. When Dash died in 1840, three years after
she became Queen, she buried him herself at Ade-
laide Cottage, and had inscribed on his tombstone:
'Profit by the example of Dash, whose attachment was
without selfishness, his playfulness without malice,
and his fidelity without deceit.'

Actually, Dash was not without faults. He was said
to have become jealous of Nero, whom the Queen
got to love because he was 'gentle as a lamb' and
particularly kind to her first baby. But Nero was soon
eclipsed by the spectacular greyhound bitch Eos,
one of the most beautiful dogs of which we have a
pictorial record. Eos was given, as a puppy, to Prince
Albert, and he brought her with him to England
in 1840 when he came to marry the Queen. Landseer did full justice to her elegant lines and magical
postures. The Queen fell in love with this enchant-
ing creature and gave her a sumptuous silver collar.
She was furious when one of Albert's clumsy German uncles accidentally shot Eos in 1842. The bitch
survived but was never the same again and died two
years later; 'such a beautiful and sweet creature, and
used to play with the children', as Victoria wrote. She
erected a monument to Eos on the Slopes of Windsor.

Then there was a Skye terrier called Islay, the
little dog Victoria came to love most of all. She taught
him to beg for tidbits, a posture he worked up into
an accomplished act in which his supplicatory paws
were excelled only by the piteous expression in his
soulful eyes. That was exactly what Landseer liked,
of course, and he put his whole heart into pictures of
Islay cadging and thieving. Islay gave him the idea for
'Dignity and Impudence', probably his most successful picture of all, then and now. Islay also features
prominently in an ingenious composition Landseer
devised to amuse the Queen at Balmoral. It shows the
terrier doing his begging act before a majestic long-
tailed macaw, sitting on his perch holding a large
biscuit, with which he is feeding two lovebirds, also
on the perch. At the bottom of the painting lies a Sussex spaniel, Tilco, with a ferocious expression on his
face. Having made a more direct approach to the bis-
cuits, he has been worsted by the macaw's beak but
has contrived to snatch one of the long tail-feathers.
Landseer had just unveiled this superb painting to
the Queen in the Balmoral drawing-room, when Lord
Melbourne happened to come in and stood trans-
fixed: 'Good God! How like!' When I used to stay for
walking holidays at Beaufort Castle a fine print of
this composition hung in the bathroom across the
corridor from my bedroom. As I soaked gratefully in

the scented suds after a 30-mile tramp up and down
Glen Strathferrar, I reflected on old Islay and his begging tactics. Did he get the biscuit in the end? Or was
the macaw as stony-hearted as he looked? If so, then
why did he feed the lovebirds?—and so on. The great
merit of good Victorian paintings is that they make
you think.

Victoria made Islay a fine scarlet collar. The little
dog grew to look like her, or she like the dog—as
often happens—but Islay did not survive very long.
He got involved in a dispute with a self-righteous cat,
and 'the dog it was that died'. Victoria sorrowfully
recorded: 'My faithful little companion of more than
five years, always with me'. But in due course there
was another Skye terrier, Cairnach, and yet a third,
black this time, called Dandie Dinmont in memory
of Sir Walter Scott. This creature, who also looked
like the Queen in a funny way, lived to be 19, and was
recorded by Landseer guarding a sleeping princess,
with a wonderful watchful expression in his eyes. No
one tugs the heart-strings more skillfully than that
old paint-bespattered monster, and the Queen liked
the picture so much she kept it in her dressing-room.
Well, it's all 150 years ago now, but the stories of
these and other pets can be found in Oliver Millar's
volumes. And of course the same kind of thing goes
on today. The present Queen's love for 'those four-

footed friends whom no bribe can buy', as Victoria put it, is just as strong. A grizzled old courtier once told me that when his wife died the Queen sent him 'a sweet letter', a whole page, typed but subscribed in her own hand. However, when his dog died he got four whole pages, all in her own handwriting.

CHAPTER 10

FROM FAIR HOOKER
TO WORLD B. FREE:
THE WEIRDEST NAMES IN SPORTS

Except for the two years I spent in the U.S. Army, I lived for twenty-eight years at my family's home in Brighton, a suburb of Rochester, New York. I attended the Brighton Grade School and Brighton High School, where the academic standards were very demanding even for a city where there was a relatively high percentage of college-educated, professional parents who wanted the best education for their children. Brighton at that time was predominantly Jewish and that fact leads to the subject at hand—sports. There wasn't much of an emphasis on sports and that suited me just fine. My classmates were smart and motivated. Nothing seemed more important than getting good grades and being accepted at a top-ranking college. My total passion was reading, especially fiction. The *New York Times* bestseller list was carried in the *Rochester Democrat and Chronicle* and I think I read almost every book on the fiction list. I'd get two or three books at the library or, when I could

afford it, at Scranton's Bookstore. I loved science fiction and
it was especially thrilling in my publishing career when I
was in charge of Doubleday's science fiction list and got to
work with Isaac Asimov, Robert Heinlein, Harlan Ellison,
Brian Aldiss, and my absolute favorite, Philip K. Dick. I
remember presenting a Dick novel at a sales conference.
My declaration that his new novel *Do Androids Dream of
Electric Sheep?* would become a classic was met with leaping
apathy as the sales manager pointed out that his previous
novel *Ubik* had netted about two thousand copies. (The book
didn't become "classic" until it was made into the movie
Blade Runner in 1982.)

I didn't know much about sports except that the stars
had names like Joe, Mickey, Leo, and Babe. I still don't
know much about sports and one of my most embarrassing
moments as an editor involved a great tennis player.

One day I got a call from Fifi Oscard, an agent I greatly
liked and admired. She was representing Arthur Ashe and
wanted me to meet with him and discuss his autobiography.
I recognized his name and knew he was a famous tennis
player but I told Fifi that I really wasn't very enthusiastic
about sports books. She said this was more a celebrity book
and Ethel Merman had told her how I had done wonders
with her memoir. Merman wasn't an easy star to work with
and I was flattered by her praise. I agreed to meet with Ashe.
A few days later the receptionist announced, "Mr. Ashe and
his lawyer are here." I went out to reception and there was
a black man and a white man. I extended my hand to the

white man and said, "It is a pleasure to meet you Mr. Ashe."
Needless to say we didn't publish the book.

One of my best friends in publishing and real life is Leonore
Fleisher, who has written columns for *Publishers Weekly*,
the *Washington Post Book Review*, and "Sales and Bargains"
for *New York* magazine. She also wrote many books, including a favorite of mine, which I edited, *The Cat's Pajamas*,
though she's probably best known for her novels based on
screenplays.

Lenore read an early version of this book and thought
the lists in this chapter leaned heavily toward African-
American names. Lest I be accused of even a tinge of favorit-
ism, she thought an explanation was in order. Here it is:

Our country has long been a haven for incoming ethnic
groups, and their surge toward Americanization often
brought interesting changes in immigrants' names.

For example, the end of the nineteenth century and the
early decades of the twentieth century saw the influx of
waves of Jews from eastern Europe. These men all carried the obligatory Old Testament Hebrew names, such
as Samuel, Solomon, or Moses, often softened by Yiddish
nicknames, such as Shmuel, Shlome, or Moishe.

But the next generation of their sons, fueled by a burn-
ing desire to become "Yankees" and pursue the American
dream, abandoned the biblical Isaac and Abraham of their

fathers, even turning their backs on Izzy and Abbie, adopting instead more "acceptable" names, for instance, Morris, Melvin, Sheldon, Stanley, Monroe, Irving, Seymour, and Sidney.

Names can and do take on a life of their own. Today, the very names those young men disprized in their headlong rush to becoming Americans are back with a vengeance, and many little boys now happily answer to Ben and Max and Sam and Josh and Jake. Also, the classic Irish name for John—Sean—is now close to the top of every list of boys' names, and so we have Sean Goldberg, Sean Rodriguez, Sean Chung, Sean Capelli, and so on.

A lot of people do know about sports and I'm grateful to the ones who contributed to this chapter. They are Bill Bryson, Mike McNew, Jane and Robert Stine, Neal Terman, Craig Westling, and David Rosenthal.

BASKETBALL

World B. Free
Lavardicus Atkins
Deginald Erskine
Dujuan Wagner
Nakiea Miller
Daryan Selvy
Rahim Lockhart
Quannas White
Shantay Leggans
Odonis Haslem
Lucious Harris
Demarshay Johnson
Tayshaun Prince
Koleone Young
Rasual Butler
Fennis Dembo
Sir Valiant Brown
Xree Hipp
Wonderful Monds
Kodiac Yazzie
The two Mapp brothers, Majestic and Scientific

And, ultimately, Baskerville Holmes, who played college basketball at Memphis State. This name was contributed by Mike McNew who added, "His mother had a thing for *The Hound of the Baskervilles*."

☺

BASEBALL

Blue Moon Odom

Lastings Milledge

J. Putz

Van Lingle Mungo

Enos Slaughter

FOOTBALL

Atari Callen

Edgerton James

Medrell Fulcher

Tebucky Jones

Zeron Flemester

James Trash

Thane Gash

Golden Richards

Mercury Morris

Algee Crumpler

Milt Plum

Fair Hooker

DeMarcus Faggins

Laveranves Coles

Zuriel Smith

Plaxio Burris

Antwan Randle El

Clettious Hunt

Gibril Wilson

Ducis Rogers

Earthwind Morland

Tezzeray Ryan

I. M. Hipp (no relation to Xree, the basketball player)

BOXING

Beethavean Scottland

GOLF

Luxchimi Gill

Marlo Galea, of Annangrove, Australia, wonders if the Fijian cricketer Bulamainavalenlveivakabulaimainavaolake-balao ever played a game at Taumatawhakatangihangakoau-auotamateaturipukakapimaungahoronukupokalwhenuaki-tanatahu on his New Zealand tour?

And finally from author Bill Bryson: "When I was growing up there in the 1960s, we heard the unsurpassable name Fonda Dicks. The best girls' basketball player in Iowa."

∽∘

CHAPTER 11

YOU LIVE WHERE?:
PLACES WITH STRANGE NAMES

How would you like to live and get your mail in Intercourse or Blueballs or perhaps the New York towns of Climax or Coxsackie? Or you could join a group of concerned citizens who live in the mid–Hudson Valley and would like to change the name of their town, Wappingers Falls, believing some people think it is an Italian ghetto. *Pazzo!*

They could just follow the residents of a town in Austria, called F*cking, who want to keep it that way—and even voted to do so in a recent election. According to an article in the *Irish Sunday Tribune*, the "150 or so people who live in the village debated the issue after roadsigns kept being stolen.... Spokesman Siegfried Hoeppl said, 'Everyone here knows what it means in English, but for us F*cking is F*cking—and it's going to stay F*cking—even though the signs keep getting stolen.'" Apparently, the name comes from a Mr. F*ck, who settled in the area with his family more than a hundred years ago, and "The villagers didn't find out about the English meaning of the word until Allied soldiers stationed in the region in 1945 pointed out the alternative meaning."

(:•:)

Here are some more place-names found in a fascinating book, *From Squaw Tit to Whorehouse Meadow: How Maps Name, Claim, and Inflame.*

    Jap Valley, California
    Squaw Tit Peak ("squaw" originated from French traders' corruption of Indian slang for vagina), in Phoenix, Arizona
    Dago Gulch, Montana
    Jewtown, Georgia
    Dildo, Newfoundland
    Brassieres Hills, Alaska
    Shit House Mountains, Arizona
    Acid Factory Brook (now Factory Brook), Rhode Island
    Dogshit Park (Del Playa Park) near Santa Barbara
    Niggerhead Point, on Point Bay in Upstate New York, changed to Negrohead Point between 1943 and 1955 (officially in 1963) then to Graves Point in 1977

(¨)

From an article called "Nice Place to Visit...Not Spell," published in the *Australian*, Tuesday, July 20, 2004: "Residents in a remote village are claiming the title for the longest place name in Britain.... The village of Llanfynydd,

in south Wales, will be transformed into Llanhyfryddawell-
lehynafolybarcudprindanfygythiadtrienusyrhafnauole." The
reason for this is to stop Spanish-owned Gamesa Energy
UK, which is looking to site thirty or so turbines up to 137
meters high on ridges overlooking the village. According
to the article, the name means "a quiet beautiful village, an
historic place with rare kite under threat from wretched
blades" and, "At 66 letters, the new name is eight characters
greater than the traditional holder of Britain's longest place
name: Llanfairpwllgwyngyllgogerychwyrndrobwchllan-
tysiliogogogoch, in north Wales."

Maxim magazine reported in its monthly column "The Museum of Found Porn": Big Bone Lick State Park in Kentucky.

Gropecunt Lane appeared on maps of London until the early Victorian period. It is now Grape Street WC2.

NIGGER HILL

"This small, insignificant hill near Causey, New Mexico, is named for a group of Negro soldiers who died of thirst there while hunting for a band of hostile Indians."

From *New Mexico Place Names, Roosevelt County* by Rose P. White.

IT MUST BE TRUE

The pastor of Little Dicker chapel in England has changed its name because too many "depraved" minds found it funny.

Pictures of men—many of them exposing them-selves—outside the chapel have been winging around the Internet and between camera phones.

Pastor Terry Brinkley has decided to rename it the Golden Cross Chapel after the East Sussex hamlet where it is based, reports the *Daily Telegraph* in London.

He said that so many jokers were flocking to have their picture taken outside the chapel that they were clogging the narrow local lanes.

Mr. Brinkley said: "We thought it better to change the sign's wording to Golden Cross Chapel in order to reduce the incidents of both private and commercial vehicles visiting the site to take lewd photographs."

Expect many visitors if you heed the advice of a real estate advertisement in *Country Life* and buy a certain farmhouse in Tuscany: Fattoria di Rabatta (paddocks). It is described as a twelfth-century fortified manor house in the Mugella Valley of important historical interest (visited by Thomas of Canterbury in 1168 and frequented by Giotto). Well maintained with considerable development potential. Principal house: 14 rooms (approx 850 sq m) with many original features. Some of the historic contents are available by separate agreement. Chapel with "Indulgenza Plenaria" (a papal right to forgive sins shared only with St. Peter's in Rome and St. Francis of Assisi) in addition to important relics.

A list of funny names of streets, lanes, and villages cited in a book called *Rude Britain: 100 Rudest Place Names in Britain*, by Rob Baily and Ed Hurst.

Brown Willy	Honeypot Lane
Booty Lane	Mudchute
Nether Wallop	Cockermouth Green
Hooker Road	Menlove Avenue
Cumoden Court	Titty Ho
Prickwillow	Crotch Crescent
Upper Dicker	Merkins Venue
Old Sodom Lane	Pork Lane
Long Lover Lane	Moisty Lane
Dicks Mount	Wetwang
Three Cocks	Swallow Passage
Balls Cross	Lickey End
The Furry	Rimswell
Muff	Dick Court
Lickers Lane	Hole of Horcum
Grope Lane	Shitterton

¡?!

As I mentioned earlier, I named my beach house in the Hamptons Lay-Me-Dune. In the UK there are some clever and imaginative house owners (mostly celebrities and newly rich), but as a rule the names tend toward the traditional and have probably been around for generations. Here is a list of the top twenty, all cozy and predictable.

The top 20 house names in the UK	
1. The Cottage	11. The Willows
2. The Bungalow	12. Orchard House
3. Rose Cottage	13. Ivy Cottage
4. The Lodge	14. The Vicarage
5. The Coach House	15. The Old Vicarage
6. The School House	16. Hill Side
7. The White House	17. The Old Rectory
8. Wood Lands	18. The Croft
9. Hill Crest	19. The Hollies
10. The Gables	20. The Laurels

Some celebrities are as creative with the names they choose for their homes as they are in their careers.

Oasis's Noel Gallagher lives at Supernova Heights, while comedian Billy Connolly rejoices in his address of Gruntfuttock Hall. Michael Jackson famously christened his home Neverland Ranch.

Less well known is comedian Freddie Starr's My Way address and actor Robert Redford's Sundance Ranch. Star Wars creator George Lucas lives at Skywalker Ranch.

By LYNNE BATESON

FROM THE *DAILY MAIL*

❋

Betsy Nolan, best friend, best wife to Robert, best daughter, best publicity and public relations agent, has a nose for names. She found the following item in the *Sydney Morning Herald.*

Business plate in Kidderminster, England, seen in 1973 by Richard Corin, of Lapstone: "Dolittle and Dalley." Richard considers the company is "probably still in existence if they live up to their name."

Sydney's distinguished jazz musician Dick Hughes still recalls with affection that business sign near the old Metropole Hotel: "I Grocock, Artificial Limb Specialist."

Returning along Old South Head Road from lunch at Watsons Bay, Elizabeth Maher, of Bangor, was struck by a large sign advertising a counseling service owned by partners Barter and Yellin. Elizabeth suggested that if conciliatory methods failed to work, "you could always try yellin."

Despite surveyors' reports and contrary evidence from along the east coast, Ducie Hood, of Tweed Heads, is sticking to her guns about Mt. Warning "where the sun first kisses Australia" and questioning Phil Jones's conviction that Mt. Imlay sees the sun seven minutes earlier than Mt. Warning. Ducie has delved into the Web site www.amonline.net.au/geoscience/earth/warning, which insists that, "The tracyandesite plug, which is the central part of Mt. Warning, rises to 1156m. It takes 4–5 hours to walk to the summit of Mt. Warning, compared to 3 hours to walk Mt. Imlay. Mt. Warning is also east of Mt. Imlay."

Holidaying in Ireland, Jackie Turner, of Bundanoon, noticed an impressive brass plate in the main street of Sligo, for the solicitors Argue & Phibbs. She wondered if they were divorce specialists.

Love rarely lasts forever but a tattoo of your ex's name or face will accompany you to the grave unless you have it lasered off. Johnny Depp's "Winona Forever" was probably the most famous regretted tattoo until he had the N and A removed to create the less embarrassing "Wino Forever."

Friends of mine got married and wanted an unusual place for their honeymoon. They discovered after research a lovely waterside cottage in Panama City. When they arrived they found the house had a name Isthmus Be Love.

FROM THE *SUNDAY TIMES*

An article in the *Sunday Times* (September 25, 2005) called
"Show Me the Way to Scratchy Bottom" cites more memorable town names from *Rude Britain,* including:

Twat

Scratchy Bottom

Tolleshunt D'Arcy

Carlton Scroop

Piddletrenthide

:)

Ellen "Pucky" Violett, a friend, built a house on the north
shore of Long Island. She was a stepdaughter of the publisher Nelson Doubleday Sr. Mr. and Mrs. Doubleday were
friendly with their bestselling author Daphne du Maurier.
Pucky loved du Maurier's novel *Rebecca,* which began
with one of the great lines of modern fiction: "Last night, I
dreamed I went to Manderley again." Manderley was the
ancestral home of Max de Winter, a Cornish landowner.
In the movie version Joan Fontaine starred as Rebecca, the
tormented second wife of Max de Winter, played by Lau-
rence Olivier. Pucky and her friend Mary "Tommy" Thomas
decided to name their house Manderley. Within a week they
had letters addressed to "Miss Manderley." When I bought
a farmhouse in Italy it already had a centuries-old name,
Il Mandorlo, because of the almond trees on the property.
Most American visitors insist on calling it Manderley.

CHAPTER 12

ᘒᕲ

HOW DID *THAT* HAPPEN?: WHEN THE HISTORY OF THE NAME IS ALMOST AS RICH AS THE NAME ITSELF

FROM THE WORLD'S FIRST INSURANCE COMPANY

Isaac Praise-God Barebone, a deeply religious preacher, named his son Hath Christ Not Died for Thee Thou Wouldst Be Damned Barebone. The son later changed his name to Nicholas Barbon, became an MD, and was instrumental in starting up the first insurance company, known as the Insurance Office, in 1667. Brendan Gill told me that the idea of life insurance was a total failure when it started up as death insurance. Success followed when someone had the bright and positive idea of calling it life insurance.

C. S. Forester (1899–1966) was a prolific and popular author best known for his novels of the Royal Navy in the days of sail. They featured Captain Horatio Hornblower, a naval officer during the Napoleonic Wars.

1st February, 1952

Dear Mr. Hornblower,

      It's a strange sensation for me to begin a letter like this; you must take my word for it that Horatio is nearly as much a plague to me as he is to you. There wasn't a Hornblower in the British Navy during the Napoleonic Wars – at least not one who attracted any attention at all. I used the name (please don't be offended) because I wanted something faintly grotesque to take the curse off the heroic things he was going to do and help keep him human. I worked for Arthur Hornblow at Paramount in Hollywood, and as a young man I was much impressed by Galsworthy's play "The Skin Game" (it dates horribly now) in which the villain (again please don't be offended) was called Hornblower. That's the best I can do about the origin of the name as far as I'm concerned – I don't like analysing too closely the way I work for fear of a state of affairs arising like taking a watch to pieces and trying to put it together again.

      I don't have to tell you that I regret, quite deeply and sincerely, that an innocent person like yourself should suffer inconvenience as a result of my casual choice of a name for a character a dozen

Mr. Marshall Hornblower
Page 2.

years ago. I had no idea then that the name would
ever come into common use. And you've no idea how
often it happens that my wife is addressed as "Mrs.
Hornblower".

I remember Alfred Stanford well, a very
able and brilliant naval officer as well as a most
capable advertising man, but he seems to have got his
facts wrong in this particular case.

Yours sincerely,

C. S. Forester

C. S. Forester.

Marshall Hornblower, Esq.

John Silbersack, an agent with the Trident Group, talks of
his own name being mangled and remembers an experience
when his father went to check in at a hotel in Morocco and
his registration couldn't be located until he asked to see the
book and found himself registered as Walter Silbersex.

THE LEGEND OF ST. ESPEDIT

In 1931, a box of sacred relics arrived from the Vati-
can on the island of Reunion in the Indian Ocean.
Somewhere in transit, the label detailing the saint's
name had been lost, and the only indication as to its
contents was a stamp on the side, reading "ESPE-
DITO" (EXPEDITED). So began the cult of St Espedit,
whose popularity grew until he became Reunion's
unofficial patron saint, whose unwritten biography
has come to crystallize the most profound hopes and
fears of the island's racial groups.

There are now about 350 shrines on Reunion
dedicated to St Espedit. They sit beside every road
junction, crown every hilltop, lie deep in the wild-
est ravines. The local Catholic Church has given the
saint the trappings of an early Christian martyr, with
a silver breast plate and a red tunic. Hindus treat St
Espedit as an incarnation of Vishnu; those wanting
children come to his shrine and tie saffron cloths to

the grilles. Some of the island's sorcerers have given the cult a slightly sinister aspect by decapitating statues of the saint, either to neutralize his power or to use the head in their own incantations.

From *The Age of Kali: Indian Travels and Encounters* by William Dalrymple.

Songwon Yun: When I was in the fifth grade, I remember our teacher taking attendance on the first day of school. All of last year's students were on her list, but the new students were not. After she read out her list, she asked those who hadn't been called to provide their names. The first of the uncalled students was a young girl who arrived that summer from Korea. She shyly announced: "I'm Songwon Yun."

To which the teacher replied, "Yes, we know you're someone new, dear, but I need your name." Timidly, the young girl repeated, "I'm Songwon Yun."

This went on for a bit, with neither understanding the other, until some of the other students figured it out.

Sally Forth: In high school, I had a summer job working at a bookstore. We waited at the end of every day for a cue to come from the manager to close our registers. One evening after the last customer, a woman in a green raincoat, left the store, the manager walked around to make sure the store was empty. In her ritual confirmation, our manager shouted from the back of the store, "All right, folks. Let's sally forth."

A few seconds later, the woman in the green raincoat came back into the shop and asked, "Who called my name?"

"Nobody called your name," we said.

"Yes, somebody just shouted out 'Sally Forth.' That's my name."

We thought she was joking until she pulled out her credit card to prove it.

☞

CHAPTER 13

~

THE FUNNY NAMES
HALL OF FAME, ALAN HALE,
OFFICIAL NAMESKEEPER

One of my oldest friends is Jack Hoffmeister. We grew up together, living two blocks apart, he on Cobb's Hill Road and I just down the hill on Highland Avenue in Brighton, New York. His father was dean of men at the University of Rochester and also chairman of the Geology Department. Dean Hoffmeister was a splendid teacher, so much so that it became my major and, under his aegis, I went on to graduate school at Rochester and then Yale. (Why I didn't actually work as a geologist is another story to be told at another time.)

When I was researching this book Jack told me about a group of men who during the late 1980s and early '90s collected funny names for their own amusement. Alan Hale was the official nameskeeper and he would periodically send updates. Jack saved some of these newsletters, often beginning with Alan Hale setting the stage for the reader's enjoyment. "I know you've all been leading stressful, high-pitched active lives; so have I. That's why I want you to just sit back, kick off your shoes and relax. I'm going to lay some names on you, sure, but it's no heavy trip. So, take a moment to get some herbal tea…. I'll wait. Ready? OK, mellow out, hunker down and, most importantly, ENJOY!"

Here are some excerpts:

Potscho Haknaser, Rockland County neighbor
Ulna Hyppolite, Rockland County neighbor
Carol Manlove Christ, PR executive
Wiff Rudd, member of Dallas brass
Hale Tuna, Turkish journalist
Periwinkle Sedigh, salesgirl at Altman's
I. Metin Kunt, historical scholar
Doris Yu Ju, married Mr. Ju
Sterling Kneebone, editor, New Jersey
Dick Stroak, late jazz musician
Adolphus Hailstork, composer
Starr Shippee, editor, Connecticut
Ariel Nicewanger, ?
Septimus Lurch, doorman
Peregrine Wortshorne, editor
Dr. Flossie Wong-Staal, researcher at NCI
Dick deButts, general manager TV station, Tennessee
King Jigme Singye Wangchuck, ruler of Bhutan
Gray Kunz, executive chef
Roger Pigaut, French actor
Lyon Roque, cast member *Miss Saigon*

Bumble Ward, PR flack

Shawna Divinity, teen-idol-obsessed jock

Magdelena Jetelova, artist; should have been a Trockadero

Dashiell Wham, high-impact PR agent on the Coast

Phyllis Fallis, bus driver

Butch Winterbottom, college basketball player

Carmela Capella, Joyce's deceased cousin

Truelove Kiss, childhood friend

Ethel Walker Smith Bush, nicknamed "Diddle"

Randy Rehr, client of Not-Quite-A-Lady Heathcote

Yirmiyahu Yovel, Spinoza-ologist

Ketty Maisonrouge, French-style PR agent

Pat Onderdonk, sister to the deceased

Lakecherette Mackadoo, assistant, Emory University

Schaphronia Flowers, housekeeping staff, Westin, Hilton Hotel

Wofford Kreth Smith, ex-chaplain, University of Mississippi

Sir Crispin Tickell, British representative to UN

Frans B. M. de Waal, anthropological author

Trupiedo A. Crump, Jr., record executive

Nickolas J. Ashooh, Paramount PR person

Nira Hardon Long, chairman of board, University of DC

Winkfield Franklin Twyman, Jr., new groom

Hortenius Chenault, dead dentist

Ditty Deamer, ask Brother Rosenblatt, I forgot

Klara B. Sauer, dyspeptic secretary?
Delbert Disselhorst, "Organ Artist" (in *Musical America*)
Dix & Eaton, PR company
Shoo Hale, a distant, inhospitable relative of mine
Choo Hoey, Singaporese conductor

Alan Hale adds a marriage note. "Hmmmm, if Miss Shoo
Hale married Nicholas Ashooh (from the last list), divorced
him and married Choo Hoey, and they kept her last name,
their names would be Shoo and Choo Ashooh!"

Also on this same subject, and I credit this one to Cindy
Adams's column: "If movie star Ida Lupino had married
restaurateur Don Ho, she would have been Ida Ho!"

More from the gang at the Funny Names Hall of Fame.

For most melodious, euphonious, and tongue-trippingest
name, the nominees are:

Sepp Ruschp Decease, ski instructor
Roxanne Farmanfarmalane, editor
Lucia Puccia, thespian

For most artsy-fartsy name of the month:

Aida Favia-Artsay, author on music
Xenophon Theophall, actor
Mr. Lawson Shadburn Yow, client's relative
Shyamoli Pyne, nobody but her name sounds like an old
song title

For most snippy and punchy name, with overtones:

Dick Trickle, race car driver
Stubie Doak, radio announcer, Ohio
Dusko Doder, reporter, USNWR

For name with best hidden and exotic meaning, the
nominees are:

Lea Hyman, pronunced "Lay'a," works at WNCN
Shi Pei Pu, Beijing opera singer
Begonia Plaza, actress
Dang Bich, General Giap's wife

!

DIRTY

Straiton Hard, Jr.
Onik Suckakian
Bonar Bain
Reema Starr
Hyman Bender

AMUSING JUXTAPOSITIONS

Maureen Poon-Fear
Midriff Billy Toast
Dorothy Green-Perrer
Fanny Smelz
Faith Popcorn

FUNNY SOUNDING

Wubbo Ockels
Jevbeep Okinis
Bartolome C. Cabangbang
Guich Koock
Batia Plotch

The following is taken from Sir Alec Guinness's memoir, *My Name Escapes Me*, published in 1998.

This past year a refurbished *Star Wars* seemed to be everywhere, but I have no intention of revisiting any galaxy. I shrivel inside each time it is mentioned. Twenty years ago, when the film was first shown, it had a freshness; also a sense of moral good and fun. But then I began to be uneasy at the influence it might be having. The bad penny first dropped in San Francisco when a sweet-faced boy of twelve told me proudly that he had seen *Star Wars* over a hundred times. His elegant mother nodded with approval. Looking into the boy's eyes, I thought I detected little star-shells of madness beginning to form, and I guessed that one day they would explode. "I would love you to do something for me," I said. "Anything! Anything!" the boy replied rapturously. "You won't like what I'm going to ask you to do," I said. "Anything, sir, anything!" "Well," I said, "do you think you could promise never to see *Star Wars* again?" He burst into tears. His mother drew herself up to an immense height. "What a dreadful thing to say to a child!" she barked, and dragged the poor kid away. Maybe she was right, but I just hope the lad, now in his thirties, is not living in a fantasy world of second-hand, childish banalities.

CHAPTER 14

❦

THE LITERARY SET

When I read *The Naked Civil Servant* I was fascinated by the name of its author, Quentin Crisp, partly because as a child my family nicknamed me Toasty and my mother would often refer to me as "Crisp Toast."

Eventually I worked with Quentin and Guy Kettlehack on *The Wit and Wisdom of Quentin Crisp*, which was published in 1984. For the next sixteen years we remained casual friends. We would talk about the movies or the theater and he had wonderful and definite opinions about both—particularly about the stars and whether they had style or glamour; he felt some had one or the other, a very few had both, and most of them had neither.

There was one star who fascinated Quentin and that was Ethel Merman. I had published Merman's autobiography in 1978, and Quentin loved to hear my stories about working with the great Merman. For example, having been a secretary, she typed the manuscript herself, with two carbon copies. Also, she insisted we include in her book the quickest way to get from Manhattan to LaGuardia Airport, a route that ran right by her family home in Astoria.

For one reason or another I was never able to get the two of them together—Quentin wasn't exactly Ethel's type of guy. But one rather offbeat occasion arose and Merman and Crisp did meet.

First some background. Someone once said to Merman (or she read it in a magazine) that doing difficult crossword puzzles was a stylish pursuit. For some strange reason, Ethel Merman picked up on this and she loved the phrase "a stylish pursuit." Every Sunday she would turn to the *New York Times* crossword. Now Merman could type eighty-two words per minute, she could memorize Cole Porter and Irving Berlin songs, or a Sondheim lyric, in a few minutes, and she sang perfect pitch with absolutely no vocal training, but she wasn't much of a wordsmith. So every Sunday morning she would call Morty, a mutual friend of ours, and say, "Hey, I got three words, let's do the rest together." They filled in the puzzle and then Ethel would call her friend Benay Venuta and help her with the puzzle. Venuta thought Ethel was a word genius and agreed that doing the crossword puzzle was a stylish pursuit.

Well, our friend Morty died and when the memorial service was scheduled, Ethel insisted on singing a song for him. I invited Quentin to come with me and he gladly accepted. He would attend almost any event—the opening of a closet door was enough; a memorial service for someone he didn't know was more than enough.

Here's the picture. A small chapel on the Upper East Side, Manhattan. Up front on one side was Morty's very square midwestern family; on the other side were the speakers with eulogies ready. Merman went first. She marched to the podium and announced in her inimitable voice of bells and brass, "This is a song for Maude, that's what I always called him." Quentin, who seldom showed emotion, was absolutely beside himself with mirth and commented, "This is going to get better."

And it did because Merman then launched into:

"The way she combed her hair
The way she danced till three
No, no, they can't take that away from me."

After the service, I introduced Ethel and Quentin. Quentin complimented Miss Merman on her a cappella rendition of "They Can't Take That Away from Me" and Merman managed a reasonable, kind remark to Quentin about his hair being a lovely cerise color. And then, out of the blue, she said, "Hey, do you do crossword puzzles?" I wanted to warn Quentin that if he said yes, he could be in for a long phone call every Sunday morning. But Quentin quickly responded, "Miss Merman, I don't read books and I certainly don't do crossword puzzles." Merman said, "You should, you know. It's a very stylish pursuit."

Richard Lederer keeps a watchful and knowledgeable eye on the use and misuse of the English language. He is the author of a number of books, most recently *Word Wizard,* and co-host of "A Way with Words" on public radio. Lederer writes a Q and A column for *Pages* magazine. Here are some examples he cites of charactonyms, or characters named to sound like what they are.

From Dickens:

Scrooge, the tightfisted miser

Mr. Grandgrind, the tyrannical schoolmaster

Jaggers, the rough-edged lawyer

Miss Havisham, the jilted spinster who lives an illusion

Other examples:

John Bunyan's Mr. Wordly Wiseman

Susanna Cantilever's Simon Pure

Walter Scott's Dr. Dryads

Willie Loman in Arthur Miller's *Death of a Salesman*

Jim Trueblood in Ralph Ellison's *Invisible Man*

Sultana by Prince Michael of Greece is a very fine historical novel and we were delighted when learned that Dorothy Fuldheim wanted to interview him. A word about Dorothy Fuldheim.

For three decades she had a television show in Cleveland. She did three live shows every day, a combination of news, analysis, and interviews with celebrities, writers, and world leaders. In the early 1970s a Gallup poll named her among America's Most Admired Women and she was certainly the most admired woman in Cleveland. When she interviewed a writer and liked his book it was guaranteed to sell a couple thousand copies in the Cleveland area, especially in the book section at Higbee's department store, where the book buyer, Claudette Price, had a huge supply of books on hand. Because of Fuldeim's clout, Cleveland was a keynote stop for any author on a promotion tour.

Prince Michael of Greece was and still is one of the world's most elegant men. He was introduced and walked across the WNET-TV set with a grace that can come only from a royal gene. Seated across the desk from him, Fuldheim gave him a steely eye and said, "Mr. Sultana, tell us about your novel *Prince Michael of Greece*." The reply came quickly and curtly: "Madam, I am Prince Michael of Greece and my novel is *Sultana*." Without hesitation Fuldheim answered, "Well, of course you should know," and then asked, "Are you really a prince?" "Yes, I am a cousin of the queen of England and fourteenth in line for the ascendancy to the throne." Fuldheim said, "That's a long way to go!" and began laughing. So did Prince Michael.

☺

In 1974 I published Dorothy Fuldheim's book *A Thousand Friends*, about the many people she had interviewed on television. Because she was recognized by everyone in Cleveland we decided to have her photograph on the front cover of the book. Dorothy was not an oil painting and although the photographer tried his best she absolutely refused to smile. (She said, "I save my smiles for handsome princes on camera.") We ended up with a reasonable likeness and captured the bright, bright redness of her hair.

When Sam Vaughan, the publisher of Doubleday, saw the jacket, he declared it "a fine example of mortuary photography!"

Gook-Sup Song, a researcher at Bucheon College in South Korea, author of a book called *Energy and Buildings,* has found that the neutral temperature of buttock skin is 32.6°C. This was cited in an October 23, 2004, article in *New Scientist*.

From Horace Bent, a columnist for *The Bookseller* in the UK: "My old friend and Diagram Prize contributor (do keep the entries coming—time for a round-up soon) Helmut Schwarzer, of Yankee Book Peddlar, writes to comment on my note about *epuise,* the French term for 'out of print.' It 'should not

strike us as all that unusual or different, if we remind our-
selves of our own expression about stock being exhausted,'
he points out.

"He adds: 'One can be tripped up by "false friends." For
instance, the German publishing term "im druck" literally
translates as "in print," but in fact means "at the printer," i.e.,
not yet in print.'"

( )

Forget the translations! I've published some pretty odd
titles in my day—*Heavy Can Be Happy, From Bauhaus to
Birdhouse,* and many people remember my suggestion to
change *The Flying Nun* to *The Nun Also Rises.* There were
two memorable submissions at the Maui Writers Conference—*Ken and Barbie's Guide to Retirement* and an MD
who wanted to write *A Parent's Guide to Hermaphrodite
Children* with a subtitle "It Is Easier to Make a Hole Than a
Pole but Is It Right?"

Think Pink! Not Fink!

Kay Thompson had a whole lot more than *Eloise*
going for her. Thompson died at the age of ninety-five
and the facts of her life are sketchy. Born in St. Louis,
Thompson, who was christened Kitty Fink, attended
the same high school as Tennessee Williams. (Imag-

ine what a superb Alexandra del Lago she would have made in Williams's *Sweet Bird of Youth*.)

She grabs our attention not through charm but by speaking too loudly, gesticulating too grandly, and one imagines, sucking all the perfumed air out of her lavish fashion editor's office, particularly when she admonishes women everywhere to "banish the black, burn the blue, and bury the beige. From now on, girls, think pink!"

Hilton Als, The New Yorker

***

Funny names? How about funny names of colors? Truman Capote did better than Crayola. Truman and his partner Jack Dunphy were neighbors in the Hamptons. One weekday night he called me, "Your lights are on and thank goodness you are home! I've been robbed! Someone broke into my house! I've called the police but I'm frightened to death the burglar may come back! Please come over!" When I arrived a few minutes later there was a police car in the driveway and Truman was in the yard. "A dreamy policeman is here and he's investigating," he said. I thought I should check it out and followed Truman into the house. Indeed there was a very tall uniformed policeman, pad and pen in hand. "Mr. Capote, how many sweaters were taken and what color were they?" I could see that Truman was warming to his audience as he responded in his dramatic and inimitable voice:

"Dozens, dozens of sweaters, cashmere sweaters! The colors? Let me try to remember." He frowned and dramatically put a hand to his chin. "Well...cerise...magenta...burnt umber...aquamarine...puce..." Truman played his one-man audience to the hilt as the policeman laboriously took notes. He was probably still on indigo as I quietly left. Walking to my car I could hear "mandarin orange...violet...pomegranate..." No simple colors like red, blue, or green for Truman but an impromptu rainbow and a wonderful performance.

☺

William Shakespeare, famously, has his exasperated Juliet crying, "What's in a name? A rose by any other name would smell as sweet..."

Yes, but would it? Picture Miss America, freshly crowned, clutching to her thirty-seven-inch bosom a bouquet of long-stemmed toad blossoms and roachwort, roses by any other name. A sweet-smelling notion?

Or would we laugh as hard at the raunchy antics of Arthur and Julius Marx as we do at Harpo and Groucho? You tell me. Would we tremble and swoon when Archibald Leach murmurs words of love into our ear? How about Cary Grant? Better, no? Does Norma Jeane Baker stun us with her unique glamour, or do the diamonds lie more luxuriously upon the satin breasts of Marilyn Monroe? Is Marion Morrison as manly as John Wayne, or do we just want to believe that the mighty Duke was born and bred a Wayne. He wasn't.

Years ago, a bright and ambitious young black woman named Karen Johnson decided a change of name might bring her the success and fame she so ardently desired. She confides to you the name she's chosen and you holler (with good reason), "Are you nuts?" But she was then (and now, as Whoopi Goldberg) as nuts as a running fox.

Were those bright stars natural roses or did they grow into roses at the change of a name. Go ask Juliet.

And then there was Truman Capote, lamenting the cruel loss of his cashmere sweaters. Because when Shakespeare scoffed "What's in a name?" he was dead wrong. And Truman knew it.

ACKNOWLEDGMENTS

Special thanks to:

Andrew Franklin, Publisher of Profile Books Ltd, who suggested I write this book.

Hugh Van Dusen, my editor at HarperCollins, his associate, Rob Crawford, and the designer, Laura Lindgren.

Michael Carlisle and his stellar colleague, George Lucas.

My literary muse Leila Hadley Luce, who shares my love of books and this book of names.

Carol Sutton, for her loyalty and perseverance

And finally Francine LaSala, who extraordinarily helped me put this book together.

And thank you to the following for their generous contributions:

Cindy Adams
Catherine Aird
Daniel Alarcón
Lisa Alther
Smiley Anders
Josef Asteinza
Michele Barber

Laura Bellon
Horace Bent
Carole Blake
Bill Bryson
Jerry Buerer
Mary Lee Burnett
Daisy Carrington

Peter Carson

Barbara Chapman

Farley Chase

Sheldon Cherry

Dan Coffey

Sherry Suib Cohen

Don Coker

George Costello

Sarah Crichton

Eamon Dolan

Janis Donnaud

Steve Fischer

Leonore Fleischer

Susan Fletcher

Andrew Franklin

Marlo Galea

Patricia Louise Thomasina
    Gibney

Brendan Gill

Michael Goldman

Jay Grelen

Carlo Grossman

Hilary Hale

Bill Harris

Elizabeth Harris

Bette Harrison

Cynthia Hart

Antony Harwood

Mary Tobin Adams Hedges

Deborah Heffernan

Frances Ingraham Heins

Tim Hely Hutchinson

David Hicks

Bevis Hillier

Penelope Hoare

Karen Hochman

Tad Hoddick

Jack Hoffmeister

Belinda Hollyer

Bruce Hunter

Susan Isaacs

Ruth Katz

Llonald King

Richard S. Klotz

Mark Lawless

Jennifer 8 Lee

Elizabeth Maher

Scott Manning

John Marciano

Ellen McClelland-Lesser

Denise L. McIver

Mike McNew

Catherine M. Melocik

Leslie Meredith

John Michel

Kate Morgenroth

Barbara Moulton

Betsy Nolan

Bryan Oettel

Theodore Butt Philip

Roland Philipps

Michael Pollan

Penny Price

Stuart Proffitt

David Rosenthal

Cyril Sapiro

Ellen Sargent

Amy Scheibe

Will Schwalbe

Helmut Schwarzer

Susan Scopetta

Jeff Shapiro

Loréal Sherman

Celestine Sibley

Anne Rivers Siddons

John Silbersack

Liz Smith

Andrew Solomon

R. Sonn

Charles Spissu

Hilary Spurling

Jane Stine

Robert Stine

Marion Lear Swaybill

Emma Sweeney

Hal Swetnam

Will Swift

Neal Terman

David Tripp

Jackie Turner

Peternelle van Arsdale

Barbara Victor

Ellen Violett

Harry V. Wade

Patrick Walsh

Craig Westling

Simon Winchester

Craig Young

David Youngstrom

Joelle Yudin